Communicating the American Way

A Guide to U.S. Business Communications

Elisabetta Ghisini
Angelika Blendstrup, Ph.D.

D1707382

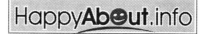

20660 Stevens Creek Blvd., Suite 210
Cupertino, CA 95014

First Printing: January 2008
Paperback ISBN: 1-60005-073-5 (978-1-60005-073-2)
Place of Publication: Silicon Valley, California, USA
Paperback Library of Congress Number: 2007941183

eBook ISBN: 1-60005-074-3 (978-1-60005-074-9)

Trademarks

Warning and Disclaimer

Authors

- Elisabetta Ghisini
  http://www.verba-international.com
- Angelika Blendstrup, Ph.D.
  http://www.professional-business-communications.com

Publisher

- Mitchell Levy
  http://happyabout.info

Acknowledgement

There are many people whom we want to thank for their input into this book. However, we won't list their names, as they shared their embarrassing moments with us on the condition that we would not reveal who they are.

Our international friends in Silicon Valley were very inspiring and encouraged us to write down their experiences so that the newcomers would be spared the same "painful" fate. We particularly want to thank our clients for giving us the fun and satisfaction of working with them and for approving some of the anecdotes in the book.

Our students at Stanford University provided us with clever insights into cultural adjustments and we enjoyed the life experiences they shared with us.

Thank you to Mitchell Levy at Happy About® for believing in this book from day one.

We are grateful for the smiling support of our children and for their patience during our long telephone conversations, sketching out new chapters.

From Angelika, a thank you goes to my new and very special daughter-in-law for her original idea for the cover page.

And from Elisabetta, a special *grazie* to my husband, Vladimir, for his constant encouragement and for his numerous (solicited and unsolicited) suggestions.

A Message from Happy About®

Thank you for your purchase of this Happy About book. It is available online at http://happyabout.info/communicating-american-way.php or at other online and physical bookstores.

- Please contact us for quantity discounts at sales@happyabout.info
- If you want to be informed by e-mail of upcoming Happy About® books, please e-mail bookupdate@happyabout.info

Happy About is interested in you if you are an author who would like to submit a non-fiction book proposal or a corporation that would like to have a book written for you. Please contact us by e-mail editorial@happyabout.info or phone (1-408-257-3000).

Other Happy About books available include:

- They Made It
  http://happyabout.info/theymadeit.php
- Happy About Online Networking:
  http://happyabout.info/onlinenetworking.php
- I'm on LinkedIn -- Now What???
  http://happyabout.info/linkedinhelp.php
- Tales From the Networking Community:
  http://happyabout.info/networking-community.php
- Scrappy Project Management:
  http://happyabout.info/scrappyabout/project-management.php
- 42 Rules of Marketing:
  http://happyabout.info/42rules/marketing.php
- Foolosophy:
  http://happyabout.info/foolosophy.php
- The Home Run Hitter's Guide to Fundraising:
  http://happyabout.info/homerun-fundraising.php
- Confessions of a Resilient Entrepreneur:
  http://happyabout.info/confessions-entrepreneur.php
- Memoirs of the Money Lady:
  http://happyabout.info/memoirs-money-lady.php
- 30-Day Bootcamp: Your Ultimate Life Makeover:
  http://happyabout.info/30daybootcamp/life-makeover.php
- The Business Rule Revolution:
  http://happyabout.info/business-rule-revolution.php
- Happy About Joint Venturing:
  http://happyabout.info/jointventuring.php

Contents

Foreword by Henry Wong

Henry is the Founder and Managing Director of Diamond TechVentures

Being able to decipher all the intricacies of a foreign business code makes all the difference in being successful.

The authors of this book, both from a foreign background, have clearly cracked this code and give the newcomers to the U.S., as well as the seasoned business executives, the key to interpreting it.

In my experience, it is clear that good communication skills can make or break a career. I came to the United States as a foreign student, and after graduation I started working in the Bay Area. I had absolutely no working experience in America. If at that time I had had a book like this, it would have helped me tremendously. I wouldn't have had to go through such a steep learning curve, which could easily have blocked my upward promotion path.

Many of the young foreign professionals I work with have plenty of business acumen; but when it comes to presenting their start-ups to American (or international) VCs, they miss a step or hit the wrong tone in their communication style.

This book explains the obvious and not so obvious misunderstandings that can occur when foreign professionals are unaware of U.S. business practices. It fills a void in the marketplace as it is the first book in English to offer practical advice and guidance to foreign professionals who—upon moving to the U.S.—feel as disoriented as they would, had they landed on Mars. With this book to guide them, many foreign-born entrepreneurs will save themselves a lot of headaches.

I wish I had had his book when I started out doing business in the U.S.

1 Why Should You Read this Book?

This book stems from our professional experience.

Over the last ten years, we have coached dozens of foreign-born professionals working in the United States. Many of them were seasoned executives who were considered accomplished communicators in their own countries. They had, for the most part, traveled extensively to the U.S. on business before moving here. In essence, they were cosmopolitan and well educated. Some of them moved within the same company, while others accepted new jobs. But once they moved to the U.S., most of them encountered more challenges than they had expected. While they previously had often been given the benefit of the doubt, as non-native executives operating on foreign ground, once they took up residence here, they were held to the same expectations and standards as anybody else.

The problem is that cultural standards are learned in the cradle, and what seems normal in one part of the world can be considered unacceptable elsewhere.

Each executive came to us with a different professional issue, but there was a common thread. They were all surprised at the misunderstandings that ensued during meetings, presentations, interviews, even during phone calls or e-mail exchanges. Despite their best efforts, they would sometimes break an unspoken rule or step on someone's toes [offend someone].

Take Jacques, a French executive in Palo Alto, who would sit impatiently through meeting after meeting, fuming and visibly frustrated about having to give everybody a turn to speak his/her mind. At times, he would storm out of the meeting, commenting loudly on the waste of time "given that we already know who is really going to make a decision here." Despite the fact that his coworkers didn't say anything, he left every meeting with a sinking feeling. He was up for promotion but knew something was wrong. Only, he didn't quite understand what to do differently.

Good managers know they have to be, first and foremost, good communicators. Good communication can propel your career forward, while mediocre communication will only hold you back despite your considerable talents. This book is intended to help professionals coming from outside the U.S. become more competent communicators in the U.S. business environment. While recent professional immigrants quickly realize they need to adapt their communication style, those who have been living here longer tend to think they have already adapted well to the local business culture. They no longer even notice their ingrained communication habits, yet their American colleagues do and are annoyed by them.

Regardless of how long you have lived in the U.S., this book will help you overcome being seen as a foreigner in the U.S. You will fit in more smoothly into the American workplace. Whether you are a seasoned executive relocating to the Unites States or a young graduate just starting out here, you know that international professionals face a specific set of challenges, as culture does play a role in how you interact with your colleagues in the U.S.

No book on business communication proved useful to the group of international professionals we work with. Indeed there are, of course, many books about business communication on the market—from general business communication topics to books specifically targeting one topic, such as meetings, or writing business English. But none of the books on the market is specifically designed just for foreign-born professionals.

While we believe that most of the principles discussed in this book apply anywhere in the U.S., we have to recognize that most of our work experience comes from Silicon Valley, and most of our clients are working on the West Coast, mainly in California. Therefore, we readily acknowledge that this book may have a strong San Francisco Bay Area bias; it is in fact very Silicon Valley-centric in terms of the conventions and mannerisms it describes. However, we believe our points are still valid in other parts of the U.S.

San Francisco Bay Area professionals like to think that "the Valley" [Silicon Valley] is the epicenter of the world, where innovation takes place. Yet, despite the strong influx of educated immigration in recent years, and despite the presence of a skilled and successful foreign workforce, the rules of the game haven't changed much here when it comes to business communication. To be sure, the Bay Area is a very welcoming environment for foreign professionals, but for all the talk of inclusiveness and respect for cultural diversity, the reality is that everybody is still expected to adhere to a certain code of conduct, a code that has been shaped by the white Anglo-Saxon majority over decades.

This book will help you decipher that code. It is based on real-life corporate and professional situations. After an initial, short description of U.S. culture which draws from leading cross-cultural experts, the book discusses a number of communication challenges foreigners typically face in the U.S. workplace: running successful meetings, using e-mail productively, talking on the phone effectively, standing out in job interviews, giving a speech or presentation to an American audience, dealing with the U.S. media, and speaking English like a leader.

Invariably, any book about cultural issues will contain a certain degree of generalizations. When we use terms such as "American," "Asian," "European," we are referring to typical behaviors or cultural norms; we realize that there are many exceptions to these behaviors, and that cultures are changing even as we are writing this book. Some expressions in the book could be misinterpreted as stereotypical, i.e., "typical

U.S. business behaviors" or "European ways of operating;" however, we use these terms simply to make certain points easier to relate to for our foreign-born readers. We hope that none of our comments and observations is seen as judgmental in any way. A final point of clarification: the terms "America" or "American" are used only in reference to the United States and do not represent Canada or Latin America.

How Should You Use this Book?

Each chapter stands on its own, and you can refer to each one individually depending on what you need. However, you will get the most benefit if you start by reading the overview of U.S. culture offered in Chapter 2. Together with a description of real-life anecdotes, each chapter offers several techniques that have proven effective in the situations described; all names have been changed and examples adapted to preserve the anonymity of our clients. In addition, the book contains a lot of idiomatic expressions, slang, and U.S. business jargon, followed by explanations in parentheses. The intent is to use words you will hear frequently, and give you a leg up [an advantage] in understanding and learning them.

The focus is practical and empirical, and the intent is to offer really actionable, usable advice.

This book does not address a number of common cross-cultural topics, such as international negotiations and English business writing. They are not included partly because there are already several insightful publications available on the market, and partly because we feel these topics deserve a separate discussion.

Finally, this book does not offer any new theory in cross-cultural communication; it is focused on helping international professionals become more competent communicators in the United States in today's business environment.

We hope this book will help you fulfill your potential.

2 Culture and the U.S. Business World

You have been to the U.S. countless times on business or for pleasure. Most times you felt as if you (could) fit in; everybody made an effort to understand you even when you were talking about topics of little interest to the average American professional, and whenever you couldn't figure out why there was a misunderstanding, a colleague would help you decipher the code of conduct at work.

But your job is in the U.S. now. You are just a member of the team, like everybody else. You are certainly not alone: today, legal immigrants represent about 8.7 percent of the U.S. population, up from 6.7 percent in 1990 and 5 percent in 1980.[1] And more to the point, some of the nation's most well-known companies such as eBay, Intel, Google, and Sun Microsystems were founded by immigrants. "Over the past 15 years, immigrants have started 25 percent of U.S. public companies, a high percentage of the most innovative companies in America."[2]

---

1. See "American Made. The Impact of Immigrant Entrepreneurs and Professionals on U.S. Competitiveness," a study commissioned by the National Venture Capital Association, 2006. For more information, visit http://www.nvca.org.
2. ibid, page 6.

Yet, the change in your status is clear: now that you reside in the U.S., you will encounter little tolerance for your faux pas, and you will no longer be given the benefit of the doubt should a serious misunderstanding arise. It will be up to you to make the extra effort to bridge the cultural differences.

This chapter will attempt to describe the most salient cultural features specifically as they relate to the U.S. business world. While we try to avoid stereotypes, we hope our readers will understand that some degree of generalization is unavoidable when trying to capture the essence of a culture in a fairly brief description.

What follows is not meant to be an in-depth analysis of American culture, but serves to identify the distinctive traits of U.S. culture, especially when it comes to doing business here.

A Snapshot

American culture is dominated by a dynamic—some would say relentless—pace of life, especially on the East and West coasts. Everybody is always busy (or appears to be) in this action-oriented culture where time dominates life. Wasting time is something that is not tolerated well, as the expression "time is money" indicates.

Pressing ahead and getting there first does matter, often at the cost of a personally-rewarding lifestyle that is more common in Europe, Asia or Latin America (where family and friends typically come first). It's a culture where work equates with success and success equates with money.

The pace of life is particularly rapid in the business world. While it is true that the pace has accelerated greatly over the last decade, it is also true that the American culture places (and has historically placed) a premium on acting quickly and decisively. As they say, "time is of the essence" in almost all professional situations. This may feel quite overwhelming for foreign professionals, who initially may not be accustomed to the need to make many binding decisions quickly.

American culture is a highly individualistic culture that enjoys challenge and competition, and prizes efficiency and decisiveness. The perception is that here in the U.S., unlike in other parts of the world, you can achieve most anything you want—and achievement is what counts: a strong work ethic brings tangible results. In other words, it's a society in which meritocracy plays a large role; it's not who your ancestors were or whom you are connected to that counts—it is what you accomplish.

Americans tend to be eternally optimistic; they smile a lot and always err on the side of being friendly. You might be surprised to hear somebody you have never met before—say the clerk at the bookstore or the cashier at the grocery store—look at you, smile, and ask you, "How are you?" or better yet, "How are you doing today?"

Don't think that these standard questions require a "real" answer. They are just conversation starters. Many foreigners in the U.S. are disappointed that these questions don't go any deeper and they talk about the "superficiality of Americans." You need to understand that this is just a formula to greet people, which is meant to be just that—a polite greeting.

In line with the optimistic, positive attitude that Americans tend to appreciate, the standard reply in the U.S. is always, "Fine" or better yet, "Great, and you?" Even when somebody is having a bad day, the most negative answer you will hear is, "I'm doing OK," which is open to interpretation, but usually comes across as more negative than positive. Brief questions are answered with brief answers.

So, how do you connect with people whose values and approaches might be very different from yours? What are the important things to look out for in a conversation, or in an exchange with colleagues before or after work? Or at a business event or cocktail party? Even casual conversations reveal a lot about cultural norms and the unspoken rules of doing business in the U.S.

A Day in the Life...

Let's listen to a typical exchange among two American professionals, and decipher what they are really saying.

A: Hi, how are you doing?

B: Great, and how are you?

A: Fine, what's new?

B: Things are really busy; I have a ton of work and will probably have to work again on the weekend.

A: Ah, I know the story. I'm on my way to a breakfast meeting.

B: I'm traveling next week, but can we do lunch sometime soon?

A: Sure, let's.

Such a casual exchange means different things to different people, depending on the cultural filter you use to interpret it.

Please write down your interpretation of this exchange, then compare it with our "translation" below.

Our translation: As pointed out before, the friendly greeting means nothing literal—it's just a nice form of hello.

Working on the weekend is a reality for everybody on the two coasts of the U.S. and some areas in between. Probably, in this case, B was trying to impress the other person (his boss?) with his work ethic.

Lunch is the standard occasion to catch up on business life, and is usually scheduled well in advance. It doesn't happen spontaneously—in fact, it will only happen if one of the two makes a real appointment, otherwise this exchange just indicates that the two colleagues have the intention of meeting again—which might or might not happen.

This conversation represents just the tip of the iceberg of underlying cultural differences that affect how business is conducted in the U.S. versus other countries.

Key Cultural Differences

In our experience, the main cultural differences fall into the following categories: time, communication patterns, distribution of power, space, thinking patterns, and individualism. These categories are not new; rather they have been drawn and adapted from the work of several leading cross-cultural experts, including Richard Lewis, Edward Hall, Fons Trompenaars, Geert Hofstede, Terence Brake, Danielle Walker and Thomas Walker.[3]

---

3. Lewis, Richard D. When Cultures Collide. 3rd edition. London: Nicholas Brealey Publishing, 2006; Hall, Edward T. Beyond Culture. New York: Doubleday, 1981; Trompenaars, Fons and Charles Hamden-Turner. Riding the Waves of Culture. 2nd edition. New York: McGraw-Hill, 1998; Brake, Terence, Danielle Medina Walker and Thomas Walker. Doing Business Internationally. New York: McGraw-Hill, 1995; Hofstede, Gert Jan, Paul B. Pedersen, and Geert Hofstede. Exploring Culture. Boston: Intercultural Press, 2002.

Time is Everything

Time is one of the main sources of misunderstanding for foreign professionals moving to the U.S. The common expressions "Don't waste my time" or "Time is money" underscore a uniquely American concept of time.

The first rule is that business schedules dominate everybody's lives. Americans tend to make appointments well ahead of time and then stick to them. Trying to schedule or reschedule a meeting last-minute is not appreciated, and could be seen as a sign of disrespect. Being on time is a prerequisite for a productive business relationship; tardiness is not just a minor fault; it is considered a negative character trait.

Missing a deadline is a major professional blunder; it is a sign of being untrustworthy. Rebuilding trust afterward will require deliberate efforts.

According to Lewis, Americans like to plan things methodically and well ahead of time, they prefer to do one thing at a time, and they like to be busy all the time. Busy schedules often leave no time to build deeper relationships. Schedules are set "in stone" and the business day looks like a series of tasks, back to back.

As Lewis points out, Americans share this so-called "linear-active" concept of time with other northern European cultures, such as Switzerland, Germany, Britain, Netherlands, Austria and Scandinavia. However, few of these cultures have such a single-minded focus as the American one.

The concept of time varies greatly among cultures. According to Lewis, professionals from Southern European countries, the Arab world, and Latin American cultures prefer to do multiple things at the same time, and tend to plan in general outlines rather than follow methodical plans. Punctuality is not really important for them, and human relationships always take precedence over transactions. The typical day of an average professional in those parts of the world is punctuated by a few important meetings or tasks, which they accomplish with a more fluid approach. Much of the rest of the day is spent dealing with people, as well as building and maintaining relationships. Lewis defines this as a "multi-active" concept of time.

In contrast, for professionals from Asian cultures, missing an opportunity today is not a big setback, as it is for most Americans. The same opportunity might present itself again in the future. That's because Asian cultures tend to view time as cyclical, as something that repeats itself.

Because of these profound differences, time can be a major source of tension among foreigners and Americans.

Consider the case of a project manager from Eastern Europe, who was assigned to a high profile technology project in the U.S. He stuck to his own (culturally driven) definition of time, and therefore sketched out a roadmap for all the major project milestones. However, he didn't produce a detailed timeline with all the team members' activities spelled out on a daily basis.

The lack of precise, detailed timelines led his boss to believe that the project was not under control. Compounding the problem, the European manager did not explain his flexible approach to his boss—he just assumed it was OK, just as it had been in his home country. But these two different concepts of time—one more fluid, the other more fixed—actually led to a serious misunderstanding.

Thinking Patterns

Americans like to discuss business issues based on facts and figures rather than on theories.

They like to break problems down into small chunks that can be solved independently with individual actions. They also don't like to listen to long explanations why a certain problem occurred. They prefer to focus on solutions.

This is markedly different from other cultures, notably European and Asian ones, which tend to see problems in a larger context and place the emphasis on addressing the issue as a whole. For example, the French or German cultures tend to address an issue based on a logical approach grounded in principles and theories, in contrast to the American preference for a more empirical approach based on just the facts.

Data, figures, incidental anecdotes always carry more weight than complex theories or detailed explanations—Americans tend to prefer simplification (which is not to be understood as being "simplistic") and, for better or for worse, appreciate efforts to "boil down" any topic to its "bottom line." This is often seen as "over-simplification" or "superficiality" by foreigners; we have seen many Europeans declare forcefully, "It's not that simple!" In reality, it is quite an art to be able to present complex information in its simplest form, an art most Americans are well schooled in and appreciate.

In the workplace, Americans prefer a model of presenting information that many researchers in the field call Inductive Reasoning: they want the main point stated up front, backed up with facts and figures.

Europeans, Asians and Latin Americans instead tend to prefer a model called Deductive Reasoning, where the results are stated towards the end, as a logical conclusion of a set of reasons. The deductive model places the emphasis on why a certain problem occurred, whereas the inductive model emphasizes how it can be solved.[4]

Take a look at the following example.

Inductive reasoning: Our market share shrank because our products are perceived as outdated. We need to invest in high-end technology features.

Deductive reasoning: The market has shifted to more high-end products, our competitors have introduced more sophisticated features, and therefore our market share has shrunk. As a result, we need to invest in more leading-edge technology.

As we mentioned, the ability to distill complex information and make it understandable and accessible to everybody is a vital skill in the U.S.

---

4. Brake, Terence, Danielle Medina Walker, and Thomas Walker. Doing Business Internationally. New York: McGraw-Hill, 1995; Minto, Barbara. The Pyramid Principle: Logic in Writing. London, England: Minto International Inc.,1987.

Speaking about esoteric topics in eloquent language—which is highly appreciated in Europe and Asia—is frowned upon in the U.S. It is important to remember that "simplified information" does not mean that the message itself is "simple."

Communication

The American culture is considered a "low-context"[5] culture, one where the meaning of a given statement is taken literally, and does not depend on the context. "Great job" means just that in the U.S., and the meaning doesn't depend on the context (i.e., who made the comment, when and how). Instead, in a high-context culture the same expression could take on different meanings depending on the context. For example, "Great job" in Italy could easily take on a sarcastic nuance, as Italians don't like to give or receive praise publicly and would become immediately suspicious when someone says, "Good job."

In a low-context culture such as the American one, communication tends to be explicit and direct, and getting to the point quickly is critical. All instructions are clearly spelled out and nothing is left to chance (or to individual interpretation). Low-context cultures stick to and act on what is actually being said.

By contrast, in high-context cultures—such as the Southern European Latin American, Arabic and Asian worlds—communication tends to be implicit and indirect, and the meaning depends on the context, as well as on who delivers it and on the body language with which it is delivered. A lot of information is left unspoken and is understandable only within the context. In high-context cultures, everyone stays informed informally.

The interaction of both communication styles is frequently fraught with misunderstandings. High-context people are apt to become irritated when low-context people insist on giving information they don't need. It makes them feel talked down to [treated as inferior]. For example, professionals from a high-context culture tend to prefer to receive high-level instructions and figure out the job themselves, and would therefore consider it offensive when American managers give them detailed instructions.

---

5. See Hall, Edward T. Beyond Culture. New York: Doubleday, 1981.

A recent article in the *Wall Street Journal* on the globalization efforts of the software giant SAP highlighted the different working styles of engineers in different parts of the world: "Mr. Heinrich advised the new foreign executives how to get along with German engineers—work hard, and impress them with content. SAP-sponsored cultural sensitivity classes taught, for example, that Indian developers like frequent attention, while Germans prefer to be left alone."[6]

Although the American preference for a direct, explicit communication style is well known, it comes with a caveat: especially when expressing negative opinions or disagreement, the usual directness becomes highly nuanced.

Sentences such as, "if I heard you say correctly" or "did I understand this well" will always precede a straightforward opinion. Learning how to politely frame unflattering comments is essential, as a direct sentence such as, "I disagree with your comments" will not win you any friends. For more on this topic, see Chapter 9.

Individualism

The U.S. is a highly individualistic culture, where who you are and what you do matters more than who your family is, and where you grew up.

As Sheida Hodge points out,[7] "the American individual thinks of himself/herself as separate from society as a whole, defining self worth in terms of individual achievement; the pursuit of happiness revolves around the idea of self-fulfillment, expressing an interior essence that is unique to each individual. It affects the way Americans interact with each other. Relationships are contractual in nature, based on the individual's free choice and preference; if Americans don't like their friends (and even families) they simply get new ones."[8]

---

6. Dvorak, Phred and Leila Abboud. "SAP's Plan to Globalize Hits Cultural Barriers: Software Giant's Shift Irks German Engineers. U.S. Star Quits Effort." The Wall Street Journal, 11 May, 2007.
7. Hodge, Sheida. Global Smarts: The Art of Communicating and Deal Making Anywhere in the World. New York: John Wiley and Sons, 2000.
8. Sheida Hodge, ibid., 2000.

Americans often think of themselves as the sum total of their achievements. Especially in the business world, personal achievement in their profession comes first. This can be a source of major conflict for foreign-born professionals, who might tend to put the team's interests ahead of their own—and then sometimes be passed over for promotion because they didn't know how to stand out.

Belonging to a certain group of people happens more by choice than by birth. Where you went to university does matter, especially on the East and West Coasts, because that gives you an entrance into some of the most powerful business networks (sometimes called "old boys networks," although nowadays women are also admitted). These networks are very hard to penetrate for foreigners who have come to the U.S. after completing their degrees in their native countries, as such networks are based on strong connections developed during years of studying and rooming together in college. They are a main source of true friendships for Americans, in contrast to the more opportunistic "contacts" (as colleagues and acquaintances are called), which are frequently relationships with professional undertones.

Power

American culture is known for being quite egalitarian and certainly less hierarchical than most other cultures—especially on the West Coast. This is true in the sense that informality is the norm, people tend to be on a first name basis even in business, and a consensus-driven style is more common and preferred to an authoritarian style.

However, this does not mean that there is no hierarchy—simply that it is not as apparent (but yes, there usually is a special parking spot for the president of the company). Signs of hierarchy are certainly less visible in the U.S.: the boss may not be sitting at the head of the table, may not be the one opening the meeting, and may not be called "Dr." or "Sir" or "Madam"—but there is no mistaking the internal hierarchy. Yet, misinterpreting the informal atmosphere for a lack of hierarchical structure is a common mistake for foreigners.

Take the case of an Argentinean manager who, invited to a business meeting in San Francisco, misinterpreted the informal atmosphere for an egalitarian culture. He proceeded to question his superiors in public, volunteered sharp criticism on the project, and acted as though everybody in the room were on an equal footing. He was quickly reassigned to another department. Respect, not deference for authority, is expected.

Space

Most Americans are not comfortable with physical proximity. They have a sacred respect for private space and tend not to hug or to be very expansive in their greetings. If they do hug, the tendency is to have a quick embrace, thump (for men) or pat (for women) the other on the back three times, and then step back quickly. A firm handshake will often do.

The standard distance between individuals in business or social settings is about 18 inches (or about 50 centimeters). Anything closer will make your counterpart feel that his/her space is being "invaded."

Space is important in that it can denote somebody's power. For example, individual power in corporations can sometimes be measured by the location and square footage of somebody's office: the big corner office with windows is much more a symbol of power in the U.S. than it is in other parts of the world (although that is not true in start-ups).

A Day in the Life...continued

The two professionals we met earlier on finally meet for lunch:

A: Great that my assistant was able to set up this lunch for today. It was the only opening on my calendar for the next three months.

B: I'm glad it worked out, because I wanted to run something by you. I have this idea and want to get your perspective. I am thinking of changing our application to make it more user-friendly, but I am not sure if there is any money for development this quarter. Do you think I should go and see Wilson about this?

A: That is an excellent idea. I really like your approach. I would go and see Wilson. But are you sure this new direction is the way to go? I wonder if you aren't going out on a limb here [taking a risk]. This may not be the moment.

B: Would you be willing to help me set the meeting up?

A: I would really like to, and maybe I could be of help in the long run, but let me look into this first… You saw from my assistant that I am booked until early next year, so I am afraid I will not have the bandwidth [capacity] to help you out.

Translation:
The lunch did take place, because one of them took the initiative to pick a time and a location—and it was the assistants who actually set it up.

Notice that A's schedule is so full of commitments that he is busy for the next three months. This underscores the concept of time as an asset that needs to be managed efficiently and profitably, as discussed earlier.

Also, notice how feedback is delivered. In this case, the feedback (from A to B) is fairly negative, which many foreigners may not realize because the opinion is delivered in a rather indirect, nuanced way.

In fact, in this case, A is suggesting that B should drop the idea altogether. Feedback always starts with a positive comment, and then comes the actual opinion (see below).

Note also how A manages to say no without actually voicing it. A has no intention of helping B and is using his schedule as an excuse. Note that he doesn't say "no" directly but softens his language to express his refusal. B, as a foreign professional, has no idea what the actual exchange means. B is left wondering: is this a straight no, or is there still a possibility that A will help out in the future? That's very unlikely.

In fact, how to say no in an acceptable way is another formula that goes this way: "Thank you… I *appreciate* the opportunity… + BUT… at this point… + *I am afraid I will not be able to…*"

Feedback and Praise

In business, giving and receiving praise publicly is the norm—any negative feedback always comes second in a sentence after the praise, and preferably in private. Prepare to receive praise about your successful work frequently from your boss or supervisor. Your efforts may also be highlighted in front of the team. American people are happy to be positive and to give credit where it is deserved and earned.

However, many of our clients report that after they are praised in public, then—as they say here—"the other shoe drops." The big BUT comes after the praise; for example: "You did a great job, BUT, in the future, you might be more precise." What it really implies is that you could and should have done better. This approach is not considered manipulative, but rather a good opportunity to give you an indication of what you can still improve. Understand that the intention is positive. The previously quoted article on the *Wall Street Journal* about SAP's globalization efforts puts it this way: "Another tip: Americans might say 'excellent' when a German would say 'good.'"

Directness vs. Diplomacy

A frequent misconception (as we mentioned before) about Americans in a business setting is that they prefer being direct and blunt, and expect you to be the same. That is not always true. While it is true that business conversations tend to be fairly informal by some standards—titles are dropped, jackets come off right away—you still cannot lose sight of the implicit hierarchy of the people involved in the conversation.

The popular myth that Americans are straightforward and "tell it like it is" is nothing but a myth. Especially when expressing disagreement, people here tend to use careful language, for example, with something like, "I see your point, and while I agree with some of what you have said, I have the impression that..." Unless you are the owner and/or the CEO of a very successful company in Silicon Valley (and we have seen some of them), you will not make friends or have cordial relationships with your colleagues if you aren't careful with what you say.

Exercise: Comparing Values

The following chart lists twenty cultural attributes that Americans value. It is a list of values that are considered important by Americans and that are frequently emphasized by most of the academic and popular literature on U.S. culture.

Now please take a moment to see how they match your values and your cultural priorities.

Please rank them according to what you think is important for you, cross out what you would not value, and then see what the differences are.

COMPARISON OF VALUES

U.S. cultural values	Your values	Your cultural priorities
Freedom		
Independence		
Self-reliance		
Equality		
Individualism		
Competition		
Efficiency		
Time is money		
Directness, openness		
Family, friends		
Meritocracy		
Informality		
Social recognition		
Future-orientation		
Winning		
Material possessions		
Volunteering		
Privacy		
Popularity/acceptance		
Accepting failure		

When this exercise was conducted during a class on cross-cultural values at Stanford University, American students consistently picked the following attributes as first on their list: time is money, independence, friends. Foreign students made different choices, depending on their culture of origin.

Why is this exercise important?

It is important because if you are aware of the main cultural differences, and you understand your reaction to the predominant values, you will have gained important knowledge that will guide your actions in the U.S. business world. In other words, you will be less likely to make career-damaging mistakes.

Is there still an "American Culture"?

There is a very distinctive American way of carrying a conversation, striking a deal, socializing, etc. that may have been influenced by the cultural contributions of different ethnic groups, but still retains its key Anglo-based attributes. As Francis Fukuyama, a well-known historian who teaches at Johns Hopkins University, points out, the Anglo-American culture is fundamentally rooted in the Protestant work ethic.[9]

Despite all the talk about diversity, and the diversity training programs that are mandatory in many companies, most American companies—especially in corporate and professional settings—generally perceive diversity as defined by race, gender, or sexual orientation. Cultural differences don't enter the picture. Any foreign-born professional is still expected to adhere not only to the company culture, but also to an implicit (Anglo) American value system.

In the business world, regardless of the recent influx of professional immigration, American culture is still defined by a set of values shaped and established by white, Anglo-Saxon men over the course of the last several decades.

The "American culture," according to the experts in the field, is, at its core, an Anglo-Saxon, male-dominated culture that traces its roots to the Protestant pioneer background of the early settlers from England. It is still the predominant culture throughout the whole country despite

---

9. Fukuyama, Francis. "Inserto Cultura." Corriere della Sera, July 17, 2007.

a large, growing population of foreign-born professionals. And, despite the fact that the two coasts—West and East—tread differently, even in this regard, than the rest of the country.

Some of the key traits include the following.

Tolerance for Failure

The ability to fail and not be considered a failure yourself is a core principle in Silicon Valley and throughout the West Coast. Failure is accepted, as long as it was a learning experience; people are encouraged to try again, and the implication is that they will be successful the second (or third or fourth) time around.

Meritocracy

This society is built on meritocracy; rising in a company through hard work (which can include ingenuity and creativity) is what matters. So if your company has an employee roster in which you are encouraged to write a short profile of yourself, you are better off sticking to your own accomplishments. You will be respected for who you are, not for what your family does. We remember the case of a Russian-born analyst who described her "influential family of doctors," which raised quite a few eyebrows in the company.

What people really don't like here—especially on the West Coast—is arrogance. Connections are as important as anywhere, but who you are and how you behave toward others will say more about you in this society than if you list all the "important" people you know and try to impress others.

You are never "smarter" than your coworkers, regardless of your education, background, and perceived status. Most professionals in the Bay Area are well-educated, accomplished, and smart.

Being Positive and Optimistic

A negative approach is very unusual in this country, even when you feel at your wit's end. It might be acceptable in France, or Italy, or Germany, to have a cynical outlook on life, but by and large, things are looked at in a positive light here; "the glass is half full, not half empty," and this, at least for Europeans, is a refreshing and liberating way of looking at things.

Consider what happened during a class on managing virtual teams taught by one of the authors at Stanford University's Continuing Studies Program. A woman in the class complained about the frustrating difficulties she experienced when dealing with various engineers to whom she was outsourcing in India. The instructors and the other students in the class spent about 45 minutes trying to pinpoint her problems and to help her find some actionable solutions. However, every suggestion was met with a negative reaction, with answers such as "This never happens to me," "My case is not solvable in this way," "These ideas won't work for me," etc. If this had happened in a European setting, the students might have commiserated with this participant and shared her negative outlook. But this attitude was highly unusual by American standards; all the students were puzzled by her behavior and were glad when it was time for a break.

USEFUL TIPS FOR WORKING IN THE U.S.

Helpful
Having a positive attitude
Being on time
Planning ahead
Working hard
Admitting to your mistakes and learning from them
Making your point with facts and figures
Harmful
Being cynical and negative
Relying on family and connections
Criticizing in public
Lacking self-confidence
Arguing

3 How to Run a Meeting in the U.S.

Picture a meeting in Shanghai. Jin walks into the conference room formally dressed; everybody else is in a suit and a tie. Jin is formally introduced to the head of the group and to the other participants, by titles and positions held. The most senior person in the room, the SVP of Operations, strategically seated at the head of the table, launches into a twenty-minute monologue about the problem, dissecting every aspect of it from a historical perspective. Everyone around the table nods in agreement. Once the monologue is over, they all take turns to speak up in support of the VP. Finally, they begin discussing other pressing items, in no particular order. Until all participants have had a chance to express their point of view, at least two hours have gone by.

Switch to San Francisco. Jin walks into the meeting; all jackets come off, and everyone is on a first-name basis. All participants have already received the agenda of the meeting via e-mail and know what questions they are going to ask. Jin goes over the main issues quickly. About ten minutes into the meeting, she switches the focus from describing the problem to brainstorming possible solutions. The meeting follows a linear sequence of topics as outlined in the agenda.

Once a topic has been discussed and resolved, Jin moves on to the next topic. When most issues have been resolved, the allotted hour is over, and the meeting is adjourned.

Most foreigners experience quite a bit of a "meeting shock" when they start working in the States. Why?

First, meetings are ubiquitous in corporate America. There is a meeting for everything, and the average manager spends up to 75 percent of his/her time in meetings. In a culture where the concept of time is linear and where schedules rule everybody's life (see Chapter 2), much of your time will be spent in meetings too (so get used to it!).

Second, meetings feel distinctively different here. They are not necessarily more or less productive than elsewhere—but they tend to be planned well in advance and run in a manner that is more deliberate. There are rules and procedures despite the apparent informality. There is certainly no patience for the formalistic, rigid meeting style predominant in Asian cultures; nor is there any tolerance for the last-minute, casual, "disorganized" meeting that is common in South America and Southern Europe. In fact, the habit of running unproductive meetings will spell your professional death in the U.S.

The focus of this chapter is the main differences between meetings in other parts of the world and in the U.S. business world.

Except for start-ups and other small companies, meetings rarely happen off-the-cuff [unplanned, unprepared] here. They require careful, meticulous planning and have certain protocols everyone follows.

Think about the meeting as a process, not just an event. The process starts off with pre-meeting planning, continues with the meeting itself (and all the mechanics involved), and ends only after the meeting is over, typically with a post-meeting follow-up.

Your role is dramatically different depending on whether you are the meeting organizer or a participant; the rest of this chapter focuses on what you need to do when you are in charge of organizing a meeting.

As the organizer, you should realize that you will be responsible for the success of the meeting. You won't be able to blame the circumstances (for example, wrong time, wrong location, hostile participants) if things take on a nasty turn. *Any* and *every* meeting you set up will ultimately reflect on your professional credibility.

> **Typical meetings:** brainstorming, problem-solving, consensus-building, progress updates, information-sharing, decision-making

Do You Really Need a Meeting?

Meetings should start with the question, "Why have a meeting in the first place?" Unless you are confident about the answer, think twice. Nobody wants to waste time on an unnecessary meeting, however enjoyable. Sometimes the problem can be solved with a simple phone call or an e-mail.

Scheduling

One of the main mistakes international professionals make is that they mishandle the scheduling process.

In corporate America, meetings tend to be scheduled well ahead of time. Walking into a colleague's office and having an unplanned, impromptu meeting rarely happens in professional settings. However, scheduling habits depend on the company culture. Start-ups, investment banks, law firms, and other fast-paced businesses have a much greater propensity to schedule meetings with just a few hours notice. Typically, you are expected to show up unless previous work commitments prevent you from doing so.

In a typical corporate environment, since schedules are locked in weeks in advance, you'll need to get onto people's calendars early. Or, perhaps you'll have to schedule a meeting at a time that may be less than ideal, but may still be your only option.

For example, a European project manager at a consulting firm on the West Coast struggled for weeks trying to meet with his superiors once he was sure he had all the information and analyses he needed in order to get their sign-off. Finally, he decided to schedule a standing meeting every Wednesday at the same time. Sometimes he didn't have all the necessary data—in other words the meeting would have been more useful on a Thursday—but that tactic solved the problem of not being able to get on his bosses' schedule!

Logistics

If you are the main organizer of the meeting, you are in charge of *all* the details. Even if you think your administrative assistant will take care of them, you always need to double-check, because it's your name that's on the line. Here are a few items you can't overlook:

Participants. Selecting the participants always involves a delicate act of political balance: you need to invite all those whose presence is necessary to reach the meeting goals, and "disinvite" anybody else.

Notifications. Make sure you send them out well in advance. Typically, that's accomplished via e-mail, and you want to be sure the subject line explicitly contains all the necessary details: meeting title, time, and location. In most companies, administrative assistants play a key role in putting meetings onto the official office calendar by coordinating e-mail invitations and keeping a paper trail [record] of all responses.

Make sure you send out a preliminary meeting agenda well ahead of time (perhaps along with the invitation) and specify what participants are expected to prepare for the meeting.

Location. Securing the right location goes a long way toward ensuring the success of your meeting: whether it's somebody's office, the conference room, the cafeteria, or an off-site space (outside of the office), make sure you give some thought to this.

Refreshments. However trivial it may seem, food is a detail you don't want to forget, as it is typical to have refreshments on hand for most meetings.

Agenda

The agenda is a list of the topics you want to cover.

Americans tend to follow agendas in a linear fashion, discussing item after item in the order they are presented; there needs to be a general feeling that the participants have reached some agreement or at least some closure on the topic being discussed before moving on to the next item. This is a distinctively different approach from what happens in other countries, where participants may have more freedom to move back and forth among topics, skipping ahead or jumping back depending on their judgment.

In the U.S., an agenda is a roadmap for the success of a meeting. Therefore, a lot of attention and energy goes into designing a good agenda.

The first step is setting a clear and attainable goal for the meeting. All too often we attend meetings without really knowing what they are supposed to accomplish.

What do you want to have happen as a result of this meeting? Give some thought to what you really want to get out of the meeting: it could be making a decision, brainstorming, getting a better understanding of a given issue, generating consensus, etc. Write it down.

Then consider the starting point for all the meeting participants; with this background information, double-check your goal to make sure it is achievable. Not having a clear objective for the meeting, or having the wrong one, is a sure set up for failure, especially for foreigners.

The second step in designing an agenda is deciding on the topics, the flow, and the allotted time for each topic. A useful framework is "what, who, when, how": what is the discussion topic, who is in charge of the discussion, when does it take place, how does it end.

See the example below.

SETTING UP AN AGENDA

What (topic)	Who (leader)	When (time)	How (result)
Intro	John	10 min	Clarify goal
Reporting problems	Guru	15 min	Review/clarify
Solutions	Usha	25 min	Describe/vote
Wrap up	Ning	10 min	Review next steps

Keep in mind that Americans prefer to spend more time talking about solutions than problems. Therefore, the list of topics and time slots accorded to them should reflect the general tendency of American culture to be future-oriented. That means, instead of dwelling on problems and their root causes, focus on new ideas and possible solutions.

Be realistic in your time allotments and stick to them: Americans have little or no patience for meetings that run late.

> **SAMPLE AGENDA**
>
> *Time:* July 21st, 10:00 a.m.-11:30 a.m.
>
> *Location:* Main Conference Room
>
> *Objective:* Decide on new applications for Intranet
>
> *Participants:* Sue, Bob, Charlie, Srini, Kurt, Philippe
>
> *Topics for discussion:*
>
> Greetings & intro: 10 minutes
>
> Review new applications available: 20 minutes
>
> Discuss pros & cons: 20 minutes
>
> Associated costs & timeline: 10 minutes
>
> Select three new applications: 10 minutes
>
> Wrap up & next steps: 20 minutes

Conducting the Meeting

Meeting Roles

How many hats do you wear [how many different roles do you have] in a meeting? Many. You can be a leader, a participant, a facilitator, a timekeeper, or a note-taker. What really matters is being clear about your own role.

If you are organizing the meeting, you will be expected to be the meeting leader—even if you are uncomfortable with this. In case you prefer not to be the leader, make sure you explicitly appoint someone to take your place. If you are fine with the leader role, but you expect some controversy, it is always useful to appoint a skilled facilitator to help you navigate the interpersonal dynamics (see managing conflict below).

If you are not the meeting leader but rather just one of the participants, your biggest challenge is likely to be finding a way to make yourself visible and heard. Americans place great emphasis on active participation, so make sure you come to the meeting well prepared and with a list of questions or points you want to make. If you sit there quietly all the time, you will be perceived as passive and/or unengaged, and your colleagues will likely not consider you a peer they need to keep in the know [informed].

Listening is also a key component of meetings. In particular, active listening is appreciated and expected. Good active listening techniques include acknowledging somebody's point or concern (*"I see your point…"*), rephrasing what somebody has just said (*"I think I heard you say…"*), checking for understanding (*"If I understand you correctly you are suggesting that…"*), checking for agreement (*"Let's make sure well all agree on this issue, are we all on the same page?"*).

These techniques send the message "I heard you" and will ensure that you appear engaged. They also make it easier for you to insert yourself into the conversation—an important trait of active participation. For more active listening techniques, see Chapter 7.

Actively Manage Participation

Positive, active participation is vital for a meeting to be productive. Encourage participants who are mostly silent during the meeting to speak up, for example, by calling on them personally and explicitly asking for their opinion. Manage those who speak too much and who tend to interrupt other participants by stepping in quickly. If interruptions become too frequent, they will undermine full participation.

Manage Conflict

Many foreign-born professionals are used to, and can cope with, a higher degree of explicit controversy than is customary in the United States; for those from many European countries, from the Middle East, and from South America, loud voices, talking over one another, openly disagreeing, etc. is a perfectly acceptable way of interacting. This, for them, actually signals strong interest in the subject at hand. Europeans and Hispanics will often not shy away from forcefully expressing their opinions.

Conversely, for many Asian professionals it is countercultural to state one's opinion openly and forcefully, especially if an issue hasn't been previously discussed.

Asians tend to be extremely sensitive about saving face and therefore are uncomfortable putting anybody (or themselves) in the hot spot. As a result, they might not express their opinions or disagreement clearly.

However, the ability to clearly speak your mind is a prerequisite for conducting an American-style meeting and will be necessary at some point during a meeting. Americans will accept disagreements, as long as they are kept impersonal and focused on the issues discussed.

So what does it take for a meeting with team members from multiple nationalities to be successful?

If you are from a culture that does not accept open disagreement, you need to force yourself to participate actively in discussions that may look contentious to you. Conversely, if you are from a culture in which speaking out abruptly and forcefully is accepted, check your tone and be sure you keep your disagreement focused on the issue and not the person.

For all these reasons, consider having a facilitator run—or help you run—the meeting if you are operating with different cultures at the table and it is your first time.

Getting Buy-In

Most meetings are about getting some sort of buy-in [agreement] into the issue being discussed. Generating consensus and getting agreement is considered a highly desirable management trait and is a prerequisite for making business decisions in the U.S., perhaps because the business environment tends to be flatter and less hierarchical than in other cultures.

However, anybody who has ever attended a few meetings (anywhere in the world) knows that agreement is often hard to come by. Here are a couple of techniques that will help you generate consensus in the U.S.:

Preselling your ideas. Most of the times, you can get agreement—at least in part—already before the meeting starts by discussing your points with some of the participants ahead of time. Try to identify those coworkers who are considered "key influencers," i.e., those who have the power or personal charisma and the connections necessary to sway other people's opinions. Make sure they are on board with you [agree to the same things], and you will be able to count on some key allies during the meeting, who will support your ideas and counterbalance any opposition you might encounter. Talking with participants ahead of time will also give you the chance to take the pulse of [get a feel for] the situation and test the waters [check out the atmosphere].

Persuading with an inductive or a deductive argument. Should you take your audience down a logical path and win them over with the power of your logic? Should you inspire them with an emotional appeal? Or should you give them a flavor of your solution up front and back it up with facts and figures? Whenever in doubt, keep in mind that the American culture is very empirical and prefers facts over theories.

Stating your solutions up front is more important than illustrating the most logical way of dealing with a problem. Don't give a lot of emphasis to discussing a problem and its origins—focus on solutions instead.

Language in Meetings

There is a code of conduct during meetings that is hard to miss, and yet it is also hard to imitate for the non-native speaker. Overall, it's important to realize that certain language habits that are considered perfectly normal or at least tolerable in many other countries are not tolerated here: interrupting, dominating the conversation, being too forceful, and being too negative are sure faux pas here. For example, a Russian-born executive had the unpleasant habit of talking over everybody else, interrupting others, and starting her sentences with a strong "No, no, you don't understand..." As a result, her coworkers found the meetings unproductive and contentious. She was eventually passed over for promotion, although she was more than qualified for the job. Communication habits overshadowed her talents.

Similarly, being too passive and acquiescent is another source of frequent misunderstandings. If you are one of those team members who sit there quietly meeting after meeting, don't voice their opinions on most of the subjects or do so in a very indirect manner, and always agree to go along with most decisions, you will probably not be noticed and promoted in the way you deserve. Active participation is especially hard for many of our female Asian clients, but they have to learn how to participate or they will not move up in the corporate ladder.

A common misperception is that since English is considered a direct language, Americans prefer to be straightforward and get directly to the point. This isn't the case during meetings in corporate America. In fact, if you pay careful attention to the language nuances, you will rarely hear American participants say, "I disagree with you" or, "This is wrong." Rather, you will hear them say something like, "I can see your point, but I wonder if we shouldn't consider an alternative solution here..."

Notice that during meetings, people tend to start their sentence with a positive note, even when there is disagreement. Only after a brief positive remark do they present their actual opinion, especially if it is negative—often starting with *BUT*.

This is a country where people often quote the saying "we agree to disagree," and are able to coexist peacefully. Therefore, direct, open confrontation is spurned, and conflict is expressed in a respectful manner. Meetings are meant to be constructive, and participants want to work toward a solution rather than analyze a past problem and assign blame for it, so staying cordial is key.

Good ways to phrase an unpopular thought gracefully and respectfully are, "What if we considered..." or, "I wonder whether you would consider..." or, "I am not sure I am quite comfortable with that..."

Sometimes simply stating, "I have a question..." opens the door to turning an argument on its head; even more forceful, the expression "I'm confused..." is used to signify that the point somebody just stated makes absolutely no sense.

A disconcerting language characteristic typical of foreign-born professionals is that they often start a sentence or a thought, and then get sidetracked and don't finish it; for example, "I think... hum... actually, I am not sure where you got those numbers... The figures you mentioned, ah... they don't really seem familiar to me."

This habit makes it hard for others to understand. It makes the speaker sound very tentative and insecure. It is possible that the speaker is searching for words, is afraid of making a grammatical error, or sees—in mid-sentence—a better way to proceed. But this is not a good way to speak.

So, if you catch yourself starting a thought and then changing direction mid-way, chances are that's a habit you need to break. Using simple vocabulary and simple sentence structure (and lots of verbs, not nouns) will help, even if it seems too simplistic to you. Another way to improve is to seek the help of a professional who can point out what you do wrong and explain how to improve it. For more on this topic, see Chapter 9.

Topics to Avoid. In general, it's a good idea to stay away from jokes—even though that may be your trademark way of defusing tension in your native culture; unfortunately, jokes usually don't translate well. Similarly, any reference to concepts, places, or people who are not commonplace in the American culture will be a waste of time and can make your colleagues feel uneasy. Other topics that tend to make Americans uncomfortable include sex, politics, and religion.

Following Up

A meeting is not officially over until somebody is assigned the task of following up. That could entail

- Sending all participants an e-mail with a summary of the meeting and decisions made/tasks agreed upon,

- Circulating the meeting's notes,

- Writing a memo outlining the next steps.

It is common to appoint a person in charge of following up at the end of the meeting, when most participants are still in the room. That person tends to be the most junior person present (although that is not always the case). Be aware that a lack of follow-up is considered very unprofessional and will influence perceptions of how productive the meeting was.

Let's Meet for Lunch!

A female executive at a consulting firm in France needs to discuss some issues affecting her department and sort through future departmental plans with the office Managing Director. Because of their busy schedules, she and the director agree to meet for a weekday lunch. The executive lets the MD [Managing Director] pick his favorite restaurant and make a reservation. She meets him there, elegantly dressed, and they engage in a pleasant conversation about their weekend activities while enjoying a three-course meal. They are both charming and personable. Business comes up toward the end of the meal. Right before coffee, she lays out her plans and asks for his feedback. He picks up the tab, they wrap up the conversation and agree on a course of action. The whole encounter takes about an hour and a half, and by the time they walk back to the office, they have a good sense of the next steps. She offers to keep him posted.

Cut to San Francisco. The same female executive meets her boss for a working lunch in his office. They let the executive assistants work out the schedule and place the order for a couple of sandwiches. As soon as she walks into the room, they start talking business. After a couple of quick pleasantries, they delve into the issues. They discuss plans while eating their sandwiches. After listening to the executive's plans for dealing with the departmental problems, the MD approves. Then he has to take a call. While on her way out, she volunteers to send an e-mail summarizing the key points of the discussion. The meeting is over in about half an hour.

In contrast to other parts of the world, lunch meetings in the U.S. are extremely business-like and tend to be very focused. Little small talk takes place at the beginning, save for some typical pleasantries. If you are expecting a pleasant, drawn-out lunch with plenty of social interaction, as is the norm in so many other cultures, you are in for a disappointment.

Breakfast meetings are very common in the U.S., whereas holding a business meeting over breakfast is virtually unheard of in many countries. A breakfast meeting can be scheduled as early as 7:00 or 7:30 a.m., and it usually involves a stronger social component than a regular meeting: typical breakfast meetings have a networking purpose or are intended to foster relationship-building.

Meetings over dinner, typically between 6:00 and 7:00 p.m., tend to have a strong social dimension and little business is conducted.

When invited to a breakfast, lunch, or even a dinner meeting, you do not need to bring a present (unless the dinner is at the host's home). Do not assume you are invited simply for social purposes: there is frequently a business reason, and it would serve you well to find out what that reason is ahead of time.

MEETING PLANNER

☐ Date, Time, Location

☐ Objective

☐ Participants

☐ Assigned roles: timekeeper, note-taker, facilitator, person responsible for follow up

☐ Topics for discussion (with allotted time per topic)

☐ Wrap-up

USEFUL TIPS FOR BUSINESS MEETINGS IN THE U.S.

Helpful

Scheduling business meetings well in advance

Notifying meeting participants early

Designing a detailed agenda carefully

Managing participation, e.g., assign meeting roles

Watching your language, e.g., not interrupting, being diplomatic, etc.

Harmful

Scheduling meetings at the last minute

Underestimating the importance of details, such as location, materials, participants, etc.

Disagreeing openly

Taking issues personally

Losing your temper

4 How to Give a U.S.-Style Presentation

A young Indian high-tech employee was regularly traveling throughout India, the U.S., and China to give a presentation about his company, a mid-size firm that provided security services all over the world. He was a very intelligent, likeable, knowledgeable man, but his presentations were long, overly technical and quite boring. His slides were so complex (at least 10 to 12 bullet points on each one) and so full of jargon, that they required 100 percent attention for the audience to be able to decipher all the words.

Like many other presenters, he thought that because he was talking about highly specialized topics, understandable only to professionals in the same field, he didn't need to make the content interesting and engaging. Predictably, he didn't get the reaction he wanted from the audience.

The solution was to rewrite the entire presentation using expressions that everyone, even from outside the field, could relate to and understand easily. In addition, we came up with real-life examples to illustrate most technical points, which made the content more interesting overall. And since the content was more engaging, the presenter was able to modify his boring tone and give the talk in a more animated style.

There is no shortage of resources on public speaking in the U.S. From books to seminars to online courses to corporate training programs, speakers and presenters are inundated with suggestions and different approaches.

Good public speaking skills are not only crucial in business, they are considered a vital skill for any successful professional in the United States. In fact, instruction on public speaking starts in elementary school here: pupils as young as ten start practicing their public speaking skills during official debates with their classmates, and they have opportunities to refine their talent throughout their academic life. In high school and college, they are regularly called on to show their work by giving PowerPoint presentations to their fellow students. They can also engage in spirited debate competitions that can award hefty prizes, and sometimes even scholarships.

An American Style?

This chapter on presentations and speeches focuses mainly on the specific challenges that international professionals encounter when giving a business-related presentation or speech in the U.S.

To the foreign eye (or ear) there is a distinctively American style to giving a speech: the essence of it goes back to a style first introduced by Dale Carnegie in the 1920s.[10] This style eventually came to dominate the business world across the globe. Known as the "friendly American approach," it relies heavily on a positive interaction with the audience. Its guidelines have become a mainstay of successful public speaking: maintaining eye contact with the audience, using natural gestures, and speaking with energy and enthusiasm about a subject the speaker is passionate about. In fact, the Dale Carnegie Institute is still very active and offers a number of excellent classes on presentation skills.

---

10. Carnegie, Dale. Public Speaking for Success. New York: Penguin Books, 2005 (first edition 1926).

Many foreign professionals have been taught the basics of this method under various titles in corporate training programs, especially if they work for multinational corporations or American companies abroad.

If you have never had any formal instruction in public speaking, you should consider attending a program offered by a local university, or perhaps joining the local chapter of organizations like Toastmasters, which will help you become more comfortable talking in front of an audience (see Chapter 10 for more details).

However, foreign professionals are not always comfortable with the "American" way of giving a speech. Frequently, these principles clash with everything they have learned during their own academic life. Asians, for example, tend to prefer a more subdued interaction with the audience and find eye contact tricky to maintain. Their main concern is to be perceived as experts in their field and be respected as such.

Northern Europeans, in general, don't really engage with the audience, as they have been schooled to keep a more formal distance with the audience. In particular, the Germans and the French often adopt a professorial "we know best" tone that places them above the intellectual level of their audience—or so they want the listeners to believe.

South Americans have no problems speaking with passion, but how much passion is too much for an American audience? And how much do they stick to the expected agenda?

Frequently, most international professionals load up their presentations with lots of text, facts and esoteric examples, making it a presentation that few Americans (or others for that matter) will have the patience to sit through.

Compounding the problem is the question of visual aids: is there a style that is better suited for American audiences?

Speech or Presentation?

For the purpose of this book, we distinguish between presentations and speeches based on the use of visual aids. We refer to presentations as a prepared set of remarks delivered to a group of people (big or small) with the assistance of charts, slides, and other illustrations projected on a screen visible to the entire audience, typically produced with the help of PowerPoint or Keynote computer programs. A speech, instead, is a well-organized address delivered to an audience that is typically larger and, most of the times, delivered without any visual, computer-based support. While this may sound like an arbitrary distinction, we think it will help clarify the discussion.

For the sake of simplicity, we will address presentations first, with the understanding that almost all the principles we cover in this section also apply to speeches. The elements that set speeches apart from presentations and the techniques specific to them are covered in a section at the end of this chapter.

Presentations

Presentations are ubiquitous [everywhere] in corporate America. If you consider their daily use as a business tool, the potential for misuse (and misunderstandings) is enormous.

The fact that PowerPoint makes it easy to produce a set of professional-looking slides quickly is a big temptation for busy executives to develop their presentation at the last minute, perhaps on a plane, on their way to a meeting. After all, they already know what to say, right?

While it's true that the industry standard for business presentations across the world today is PowerPoint, it's also true that visual aids don't always support the speaker (as the word "aid" suggests). In fact, sometimes they detract from the speaker's effectiveness because they are not carefully chosen and distract from the message.

There might have been a time when writing your presentation on a plane on your way to a meeting was OK. But it's not a smart choice, especially not in the U.S. Don't risk being unprepared. The first principle of a successful presentation is for the speaker to know his/her subject very well. That applies to everyone (including Americans), but especially to foreigners because of the language "handicap."

It's not necessarily a matter of competence: you may be a great presenter in your home country, but your style may not be as effective with an American audience. In general, foreigners are less likely to be successful when giving a presentation without being fully prepared, maybe because they are afraid that their language deficiencies will show.

This means that the presentation has to be fully outlined and developed before flight time. The only good thing to do on the flight is to go over the presentation one last time and mentally practice the delivery—again.

Foreign-born professionals face specific challenges that can undermine their effectiveness as presenters. These challenges fall into three main categories: content, visual aids, and delivery.

Content

Content is obviously specific to your industry, but there are some general cultural rules that apply. To make sure you make smart choices about the content of your presentation, we recommend following a structured approach: understand your audience, define your goals, and sketch out an outline. Don't start writing before you know whom you are talking to and what you want them to do.

Analyze Your Audience—Cultural Considerations

When thinking about an American audience, keep in mind that there are general cultural characteristics that apply to most American audiences: a preference for solutions over problems, an orientation to the future rather than the past, a preference for brevity and simplicity—and for lots of stories and examples to clarify the main points.

Americans prefer to talk about solutions rather than problems. So, the first rule is to emphasize your solution to a given problem. Dwelling on the specifics of a problem or exploring the origins of the issue might be the preferred approach in Europe or South America. But if you do so here, you will lose your American audience within the first ten minutes.

That's what happened to a German manager who was summoned by his American boss to explain why a product launch had been delayed. He prepared a presentation explaining all the reasons why the delay occurred. But instead of placating his boss, these explanations unnerved him even more. All the boss really cared about were the manager's plans for dealing with the delay—when would the product launch finally take place? The boss was willing to listen to the reasons for the delay only insofar as they impacted the plan of action, but not a minute more. Our German manager compounded the problem with his presentation instead of helping solve it. He gave his boss the impression he was trying to cover up his own incompetence, or passing the buck to someone else [make someone else responsible], rather than focusing on how to solve the problem. He should have quickly covered the reasons for the delay and then focused on his plans for the future launch.

This emphasis on solutions stems from a general cultural orientation towards the future rather than the past. The future is what matters. Americans do not have a strong sense of history and aren't as intrigued by the past as they are by the future.

Another principle to remember is that of simplicity: try to simplify the issues at hand rather than dwelling on their complexity. Keep it short. Foreigners frequently have a tendency to include as many details as possible when explaining an issue. But again, Americans have very little patience for a great amount of details. They want to get to the point quickly and discuss what needs to be done (see below for more details).

The local political climate should also be taken into account, and our advice is to avoid any political reference, since regional values differ significantly throughout the U.S. We are reminded of a client of ours, a liberal left-wing European female executive living in the progressive circles of the Bay Area, who slipped a number of ironic remarks about the current Bush administration into her training program at a company in the Midwest. She received a chilly reaction to her presentation, and was officially rebuked by HR later—even though everybody found the content of her training very good and relevant. This experience goes to show that it's always a good idea to play it safe and avoid controversial topics in your presentations or workshops.

In-Depth Audience Analysis

Beyond being aware of general cultural characteristics, we recommend conducting a thorough audience analysis of the particular group of people you are facing: some industries are well known for being more conservative than others (e.g., financial services and health care are notoriously more buttoned up than technology and media). If you are not presenting within your company, we recommend checking with the organizer of the event about the make-up of the audience (demographics, educational level, knowledge of the subject, possible biases, etc.), and adjusting your presentation accordingly.

We have been at events where the presenter had no clue [didn't know] of the educational background of the audience and didn't endear himself by patently talking down to us, saying things like, "I can't really go into detail, this is a really complicated issue." You can guess what kind of impression that made on his audience.

Also consider the positional power of the members of your audience: How much do they know about the subject already? Do they have strong opinions about it? Are they likely to be opposed, indifferent, or in favor of what you are presenting?

In essence, every time you write an outline, ask yourself:

- *What does this mean to the audience?*

- *Why do they care about it?*

- *What do they know already?*

- *How will they benefit?*

If you can't answer these questions, throw it away and write a new one.

AUDIENCE CHECKLIST

Who is your audience?	What does your audience prefer?
☐ Decision makers ☐ Opinion leaders ☐ Line/middle managers ☐ Other	☐ Concepts/theories ☐ Facts/analysis ☐ Action/recommendations ☐ Presentations ☐ Informal discussions
How much does your audience know/what do they think?	**How is your audience likely to react?**
☐ Very concerned/ somewhat concerned ☐ Neutral ☐ Thorough knowledge ☐ Limited knowledge ☐ Willing to change ☐ Resistant to change	☐ Agreement ☐ Disagreement ☐ Neutral

Define Goals

Know why you are giving this talk and be specific when defining goals. Do you want to change the way your audience thinks about a certain issue, convince them that your solution is the best one, spur them to action...

Business communication is all about results, and there is truth to the old adage: "How will you know if your presentation has been successful if you didn't have a clear goal?"

Your goal could range from informing your audience, to persuading it, to compelling it to take action...whatever you goal is, it will shape your content, and you really should only include what will help you achieve it.

Make an Outline

Most speeches and presentations in the U.S. have a fairly predictable structure—opening, body and close—which will be your guide when you start sketching out your outline. There is a saying here that characterizes how a presentation should flow: tell them what you are going to tell them, tell them, and then tell them what you told them.

Opening

A story or a personal anecdote is often a good choice to pique the audience's attention and provide an interesting introduction to your main topic. It could also be a statistical fact, or some other type of *factoid* that will get your audience interested. You can talk about something relevant that happened in the industry to build a connection and show you understand your audience. If you happened to network ahead of time and were able to connect with some of the audience members and get their names, it is good to weave that into your opening; your audience will appreciate it.

Often presenters tend to neglect the opening and simply start with a very conventional sentence, such as: "My name is Joe (or Mary) and I would like to talk about X with you today." While there is nothing wrong with such a common introduction, everybody has heard it a million times already, and therefore it tends to come across as fairly flat and uninspiring—the opposite of what you want to achieve. We find that our foreign-born clients have a wealth of experiences that are new to the audience and that would hold its attention.

Body

Some presenters prefer to sketch out an outline of bullet points which they will later translate into slides, while others prefer to sketch out storyboards (i.e., a series of very preliminary slides, sometimes just with a title, a main point, and a simple graph) arranged in the right sequence. All the details are filled in at a later stage.

Whatever your preference, we believe that your main task will be deciding on the logical sequence of ideas. While there are many approaches to organizing the content of your presentation, typically, you will have to choose between an inductive way of presenting information or a deductive way of presenting it (see Chapter 2 for more details). What does this mean in practice?

The inductive model is also called "top down" because it starts with the solution and backs it up with evidence. This is a more engaging way of presenting material for American audiences. Many people nowadays like to hear the conclusions up front, and only then do they want to see how this conclusion was reached.

By contrast, the deductive model is also called "bottom up" as it starts with the problem and leads the listener to the solution. Inductive models place the emphasis on *how*, whereas deductive models emphasize the *why*. This approach is more common in the scientific and medical fields.

An example might be the following one.

Inductive: Our market share has dropped dramatically because the market overall has shrunk and our products are not very competitive any longer. We should introduce new, state-of-the-art products.

Deductive: The market has changed as a result of economic uncertainty, changes in consumers' preferences, and the perception is that our products are not very competitive because of outdated features. Therefore our market share has dropped dramatically. Only by investing in new, state-of-the-art products can we regain our market share.

You will need to decide which kind of approach your audience prefers. In general, Americans prefer listening to *how* a certain solution is supposed to work rather than to *why* that particular solution is the best one at hand. Therefore, the inductive model tends to be more popular.

This model is also called the Pyramid Principle[11] in many consulting firms: envision a pyramid with the solution at the top, gradually leading down to more in-depth information. In journalistic terms, it is instead

---

11. Minto, Barbara. The Pyramid Principle: Logic in Writing. Minto International Inc., London: England, 1987.

called the "inverted pyramid": think of an article with a sentence at the top that captures all the essential information and less important details at the bottom.

The definitions may sound confusing, but the principle is clear: start with the solution/most relevant information and leave the details (i.e., evidence, premises) for later.

Whatever your choice, always keep the KISS rule in mind: Keep It Simple, Stupid. This well-known rule is just a reminder to make sure your content is easy to understand.

The biggest mistake you can make is to try to impress your audience members with your oratory skills, rather than talking to them with one clear message and leading them to understand it.

At the risk of oversimplifying the problem, stick with simple language. That applies to vocabulary as well as concepts.

- Use simple words as much as possible, rather than high-sounding expressions, to show off your skills of higher thinking.

- Use verbs rather than nouns (see Chapter 9).

- Avoid jargon. Even if you assume everyone is familiar with it, you may have listeners who are there to learn and who would not understand you.

- Beware of acronyms. While probably everyone in Silicon Valley knows what WYSIWYG[12] is (do you?), acronyms can be very confusing for those not "in the know."

- People love sound bites and headlines, so see if you can put in a few into your presentation. For example, an international professional might say: "Every participant needs to contribute in order to be admitted to the negotiations." Instead, Americans would say: "We are going to use the 'pay to play' principle."

---

12. What you see is what you get.

Being brief is always appreciated, so pay particular attention to the total length of your presentation. Many public speaking programs promote the notion that the average attention span in the U.S. is a maximum of 30 minutes,[13] after which attention naturally drops. Actually, by culture and by habit, Americans have absolutely no patience for long, rambling presentations. And remember that going beyond your allotted time is a cardinal sin here. You can be sure that somebody *will* cut you off soon after your time is up (sometimes politely, sometimes abruptly), whether or not you have finished your presentation. And they will remember you didn't play by the rules.

Recently, we gave a workshop at an international conference and were scheduled to start immediately after a visiting southern European presenter. He went over his allotted time by 30 minutes, and while the organizers were too polite to cut him off, he will probably not be invited again.

Closing

Often you will hear a good presentation, but at the end you are left wondering what to do with the information you just received. The most common thing is to put the presentation into a drawer and leave it there, forgotten. A good way to close is by providing a quick summary of the main points discussed, i.e., "tell them what just you told them." However, a better way of closing a presentation is to have a call to action: "Now that you know XYZ, here is what I would suggest you do next."

There should be action items and practical steps for the audience to take home.

Visual Aids

What materials should you prepare for your presentation?

As mentioned before, PowerPoint seems to be the current global industry standard across the business world. Therefore, it is most likely

---

13. Lewis, 2006, page 72.

that you will also use PowerPoint slides for your presentation, and there is nothing wrong with this, as long as they are clear and useful.

However, lately we have noticed a backlash: "PowerPoint Hell," as the abuse of slides has become known in Silicon Valley (too many slides, not enough originality). As a result, a few high-tech companies have now explicitly prohibited the use of PowerPoint slides for internal meetings.

So, watch out for the most frequent mistakes that have come to define PowerPoint Hell.

Squeezing too much information onto a single slide. Too much text, too many numbers, too many images, too many bullet points. As a consequence, your audience will try to read your slide but tune you out in the process. Remember that a slide is only meant to *support* you as a speaker, not overpower you. Each slide should have one message—just one message, clearly expressed in the title. Anything that doesn't support that message should be left out.

Remember also that your audience will be able (or will want) to read only a limited number of words or figures per slide. As a general rule, no more than six bullet points per slide and six words per bullet.

If your slides are confusing, or your point is not clear, you are not likely to get a polite, distant response as you might in other parts of the world. You will get a blunt "So what?" question.

Foreign-born professionals are typically taken aback by what they perceive as an abrupt remark, and they frequently take it as a display of ignorance, which it definitely is not. Expect to be challenged when you are long-winded or beside the point. There is no loss of face involved in a question like "So what?" It's just a request for clarification and a hint that you should get to the point.

Too many slides. When preparing your materials, think about the length of your presentation and the time you have available. An old rule of thumb suggests a minimum of one minute per slide if it's a simple slide, and two minutes for a more complex explanation. That assumes a fairly static delivery with no interruption.

But the norm now tends to be in favor of a more interactive discussion, even during presentations (depending on the size of the group: the smaller the group, the more interaction). Therefore, it is wise to assume that the discussion will take more time than expected. And that means fewer slides. A good rule is that a manageable number of slides for most presentations is between ten and twenty, according to Guy Kawasaki,[14] a popular author for budding entrepreneurs. However, if you have quite a lot of information to get through, it is still preferable to split up the information into several slides rather than to cram it all into a few, illegible charts.

Delivery

As we all know, having the right content is only half of the equation. The other half is delivering it with conviction and enthusiasm. In other words, it's not only what you say that matters, it's also how you say it.

The first rule of the game is *not* to read your slides aloud. Many executives (foreign-born or not) use their slides as a crutch and are literally glued to their PowerPoint presentation. For most nonnative speakers of English, "reading" their slides might seem the safest option as it doesn't require them to think on their feet or prepare much ahead of time.

But reading your slides, or reading your script, invariably comes across as artificial, ineffective, and incredibly boring. If you do that, don't be surprised when people get up and leave, as your presentation will be considered a waste of their time.

Prepare

Invest in preparation and practice.

Many of the U.S. executives whom you see on stage make it look so easy, but they have actually spent many hours practicing, often with a coach (a fact they don't always disclose).

---

14. Kawasaki, Guy. The Art of the Start. Penguin Group, 2004.

Do prepare a script if you feel you need to. But don't read directly from it. Rather, convert it to a set of notes or bullet points. This way you will remember all the key words and the expressions you cannot afford to mispronounce, and beyond that, you will come across as more energetic and genuine.

How You Come Across

A presentation is always a bit of a performance, so let's look at the elements of your body language that can make a difference in how you are perceived:

Energy level. Americans like high-energy, enthusiastic presenters. High energy projects a sense of self-confidence and optimism that plays well in the eternally positive American culture. Make sure you "psyche" yourself up [adopt a positive mind set] and start your presentation on a high note. Even if you are a bit unsure or intimidated by the situation, do your best to conquer your fears and get into "performance mode." It will pay off in spades [it will be worth it] in terms of your credibility. A humble, understated "stage presence" will not play well here.

Voice. Many foreigners tend to speak in a soft voice as a result of either being insecure when speaking in a foreign language or having been raised to not stand out too much. We have seen this with many of our clients, especially (but not only) with Asian women. Big mistake! Americans already struggle to understand you because of your accent or because of your sometimes unusual word choices, and then, in addition, you are forcing them to strain themselves just to hear you!

Try to make an extra effort to raise your voice; project your voice strongly from your chest, enunciate words fully and clearly, and keep your volume up at the end of the sentences, when your voice typically tends to taper off.

Sometimes we have witnessed the opposite situation, i.e., one in which foreigners (especially if from Southern Europe or from Latin America) speak too loudly and perhaps too forcefully. This may make your listeners feel uncomfortable, and the obvious advice is to tone it down a bit—although we'd rather see you being too forceful than too fragile.

Eye contact. The standard advice is to divide the room into quadrants and focus on individual participants while expressing a *complete* thought. This is great in theory but hard to do in reality, so you will have to practice to get it right.

Maintaining eye contact is typically more of a problem for Asians or Latin Americans, who may have been brought up to view direct eye contact as a sign of disrespect. The opposite is true in Western cultures: lack of eye contact is viewed as a sign of untrustworthiness. So practice direct, sustained eye contact, preferably with one participant at a time, focusing on each quadrant of the room.

A good technique here is to identify an "ally" or friend in the audience: somebody who seems to like you and seems to approve of what you are saying (perhaps by nodding vigorously). Circle back to that person every now and then. This is sure to boost your self-confidence even in front of the most skeptical audience!

If you have someone in the audience who asks a lot of irritating questions, try this technique: smile, answer the question, then deliberately look away from that person, and finish your thought focusing on somebody at the other end of the room. That way the naysayer will need to make an extra effort to get your attention—which hopefully will act as a deterrent!

Smiling. For many of us who didn't grow up here, smiling a lot when presenting feels unnatural. However, smiling helps you win the confidence of the audience. Even if the subject is serious, try to put in a smile. It will make you look relaxed and confident—and the audience will like you more!

Gestures. This is one area in which Southern Europeans excel! Gestures are good as they add visual emphasis to your speech. Make sure you keep your arms and hands moving upwards of your waist, so people keep looking at you and what you are saying and are not focusing on your movements. Make big gestures (i.e., arms wide), as you have the whole stage for yourself.

Stance. Stand with your feet hip-width apart, your weight balanced evenly on your legs in a fairly stable position with minimal walking around… you have certainly heard all of this already. It still holds true, so practice your stance.

After reviewing all these techniques, one final thought: take our advice with a grain of salt. Recently, we attended a speech given by a famous journalist at Stanford University. He wasn't well dressed, he leaned on the podium, then he moved around a lot on the stage—any presentation coach would have been aghast. However, once he started speaking, no one paid any attention to his movements. The entire auditorium was spellbound by what he was saying and the passion he put into his words.

After all, powerful content is the most important part of your presentation.

Mechanics

You want to check all the details in advance: room layout, podium lights, LCD projector, cables to your laptop, mike, acoustics. It's important to check ahead of your speech in order to avoid last-minute surprises. Remember to bring a printout of your presentation, just in case. Quite a few presenters we have seen over the years had problems with their computer equipment, but they had a copy of their slides in their hands and were able to pull off convincing presentations anyway, because they were prepared.

Rehearse

Rehearsing is imperative for everybody, but especially for foreigners. And we mean rehearsing out loud, preferably with a friend or colleague, but if nobody is available, the mirror will do. The best would be for someone to video tape you so you can hear and see yourself and correct any annoying habits.

How many times should you rehearse? The standard advice is three to five times: anything less won't get you fully prepped, and anything more will make you sound too artificial.

If you don't have the time to rehearse thoroughly, make an effort to practice at least the opening and the close of your presentation, as crucial impressions are formed quickly—at the beginning and at the end. Rehearsing your lines will also help minimize your accent and help you make sure you pronounce most words correctly, which will make it easier for the audience to understand you.

Questions and Answers

Questions and answers (Q&As) are a very important part of your presentation. In fact, they are a barometer of your audience's reaction. Many international professionals, however, are either terrified by the prospect of handling a Q&A session or are looking forward to the opportunity to silence the opposition. Both attitudes are a recipe for disaster. Understand that Q&As are a natural component of any presentation or speech in the U.S.; in fact, a lack of questions at the end of a speech typically means the audience either didn't understand it or was not engaged.

Handling Q&As smoothly does take some preparation: for example, we always advise our clients to try to anticipate as many questions as they think might be asked, and prepare some bullet points to answer them with ease.

But the truth is, you can't predict all of the questions. So take a deep breath, relax, and hold the fire—that's right, do not fire back. Always respond in a gracious way. Being defensive will only make things worse.

The techniques that are generally recommended and that do work pretty well are to listen carefully to the question, to breathe, to pause, and to rephrase the question if necessary (it helps clarify the point and buys you time to think). Be thoughtful with your answer; try to keep it simple and brief. If you don't have an answer or would prefer to discuss the issue separately, offer to meet privately with the person who posed the question.

A mistake that many foreigners make—especially Europeans—is to fire back an answer quickly with a tone of superiority, which will be seen as rude or not thoughtful enough. Even if you think you are getting a great deal of difficult questions from a couple of participants, the best way to deal with them is to very politely answer their questions and offer to talk with them after the presentation. It is perfectly acceptable in the U.S. to say you don't have all the facts right now but will get back to them when you do.

Asians tend to make the opposite mistake, i.e., answering a question in a very indirect way. We remember a situation in which a Japanese consultant working in the Bay Area was asked whether it was true that a well-known Japanese businessman was overbearing and very difficult to deal with. He replied that everybody is the product of his childhood, and therefore, he inferred that the businessman's parents must have been very demanding. The audience went "Huh?" This roundabout answer irritated the audience and didn't win him any points with his colleagues, either.

Speeches

In an auditorium at Stanford University, during a seminar on public speaking for students enrolled in the Graduate School of Business, several students proceeded onto the stage to introduce themselves as a way to practice their public speaking skills. An endless series of standard introductions such as "My name is Joe, I come from Montana, I got my undergraduate degree from Yale, and I would like to share with you my passion for x" elicited a lot of yawns and visible signs of boredom from the audience. Then a foreign student took to the stage. He started on a different note, and everybody fell silent: "September 19th, 2002, gunfire shots throughout the streets of Abidjan, Cote d'Ivoire. That day marked my life as it was the beginning of my family's exile…"

You could hear a pin drop in the vast auditorium. The audience was listening, captivated.

Why?

It's the power of personal stories and interesting anecdotes.

Personal stories help you anchor the narrative with some kind of image your audience can visualize and retain as you progress through your speech. And most foreigners are likely to share stories that, by definition, are probably not mainstream American, which can make your speech more intriguing to the average American audience. However, you need to be careful not to stray too far from the common ground, or your audience might not understand you altogether.

As for the body of the speech, the question is always how to organize your thoughts and ideas in a way that makes it easy for the audience members to follow you and keeps their attention level high. Start by selecting only what's relevant to your overall message and have a clear roadmap (e.g., an outline), so your audience knows where you are going. Try to limit your content to three main points, as that will make it easier for your audience to follow you.

Finally, close with a recap of your main points and a call to action.

As for the delivery of your speech, it is highly recommended NOT to read from your script, if you have one. (Unless you are Steve Jobs reading his—now famous—Stanford University graduation speech in 2005. He can get away with it.) In fact, we recommend not having a full-blown script at all, otherwise you may end up memorizing it and panicking if you can't remember certain lines during the speech itself.

Most people do well working with a list of bullet points—some more scripted, some less—to guide them through the speech.

Others use a series of cards with a key thought on each, which they use just as a starting point for expanding and improvising. Others yet use the image of a circle, with key thoughts/icons flowing from one point to the next.

Whatever your technique of choice, you will have to strike a happy medium between preparation and improvisation.

Improvising a speech is very tricky for everybody, and especially for foreign-born professionals—and we certainly do not recommend it.

Again, invest in preparation, know your strengths as a speaker, and rehearse a couple of times at least.

And remember to enjoy it!

USEFUL TIPS FOR GIVING A PRESENTATION IN THE U.S.

Helpful
Having a clear message, stated up front
Using simple language
Relying on a few, intuitive visuals
Being energetic and passionate about your ideas
Emphasizing the future rather than the past
Understanding the cultural characteristics of your audience
Harmful
Putting audience into Powerpoint hell (abuse of visuals)
Improvising content
Burying the lead concept, i.e., stating your key ideas at the end of the presentation
Not rehearsing
Being verbose
Using jargon, acronyms
Being too low key and hesitant

MOST FREQUENT TYPES OF PRESENTATIONS

Progress report: The general rule of thumb is to get all the bad news out quickly. Then focus on your plan for the future. State the facts and don't try to find excuses; this would be misunderstood as an attempt to cover up your mistakes.

It is better to admit to a failure and show you have learned from it. So be honest in your assessment and quickly move on to what you will do differently now and the next time.

Sales pitch: Americans like a direct sales approach in which you highlight the benefits of a certain product or service up front, in a very explicit way—it's called the "hard sell." A sales pitch is really focused on convincing your audience that what you are describing is the best possible option for them.

This explicit selling approach is likely to feel uncomfortable to many international professionals; however, a more subtle, indirect approach will simply not work well here.

Pep talk to rally the troops: This is a very American expression that refers to a motivational speech for the team. The key word here is motivation. Since you can't count only on your positional power to impose a new direction or new rules on people who work for you—it would clash with the U.S. style of managing by consensus—you need to convince your team that what you are suggesting is the best way to go.

This is the only time we advise you to emphasize *why* rather than *how* it will work. For example, when instituting a cost-cutting program, a department manager took the time to explain to her team exactly what the costs were and why they needed to be reduced. Had she been talking with her boss, she would have shifted gears right away to show how the cost-cutting program would be implemented.

Update to your boss: The preferred way to update your boss is to do so quickly and directly. In essence, the same principles used for a progress report apply here: good (or bad) news out quickly, admit your mistakes honestly, and focus on the future.

Presenting at an executive or partners' meeting: Be very sensitive to the majority opinion. Always try to build consensus before your presentation, perhaps by winning over key constituencies ahead of time, in order to avoid any surprises. And be sure to use very careful language that is not likely to ruffle any feathers [upset anybody].

It's not a good idea to contradict somebody in public or to state a controversial opinion openly and forcefully.

A professor of electrical engineering from Eastern Europe—considered a worldwide authority in his niche and hired as a consultant on a high-profile project—dared to challenge the majority opinion openly at a conference of the Institute of Electrical and Electronic Engineers; even though he was ultimately right, his behavior did not win him friends in the long term.

5 How to Hold Productive Phone and Conference Calls

An executive at a consulting firm in southern Europe is getting ready to start an important conference call to discuss a project update. Five team members are scattered throughout Europe (all in the same time zone) and have been informed about the call just yesterday.

At the beginning of the call, the executive greets everybody by name as they join in; a few of them are a couple of minutes late. While waiting, he engages in some small talk, inquiring about the team members' weekend activities, remarking on the latest soccer match, and teasing them about recent successes or failures. As the call gets underway, the executive reminds everyone of the topic of the conference call. Then he proposes an agenda and moves to the first point. He asks for the opinion of the team member who is considered an expert on the subject. Other participants throw in their ideas and opinions, their voices often overlapping. Throughout the call, they enjoy a few jokes and personal remarks. The call is over when time is up. Even though they haven't covered everything they wanted to, they feel the call was productive because the most important issues were solved.

A couple of people agree to follow up on some of the points, and everybody decides to continue the discussion at a meeting later in the week.

Switch to the U.S. Same company, similar situation. The team members are in different time zones throughout the country and haven't seen each other in a while. The call has been scheduled about a week before via e-mail. All team members received a copy of the agenda ahead of time, were asked to prepare their thoughts, and to contribute their opinions on some specific points, depending on their areas of expertise. At the beginning of the call, they all introduce themselves, using their first names.

As the call gets underway, all participants have a copy of the agenda in front of them. The executive leads the call and introduces the first point. Then the subject expert takes over, presents her opinions and proposals, and the executive assigns tasks to various team members. A participant chimes in [adds his comments] to remind the others of the time and suggests they move to the next topic. Before the end of call, they cover all the topics, agree on responsibilities for follow-up tasks, and pick a date and time to reconvene. By the end of the day, an appointed team member sends out a summary of the call and a reminder of the next steps. Now the call is officially over.

A lot of business is conducted over the phone in the U.S. In fact, phone interactions have probably become more common than in-person meetings for members of a team. Mastering effective phone manners is a vital skill for a professional in the U.S. Unlike in other countries, the phone is considered just a work tool here, not a means for staying connected. Productive phone calls during business hours are always preferable to calls that are just "pleasant." That means little time is devoted to small talk and just "catching up" at the beginning of a business conversation.

Many of our clients are very self-conscious of their "phone manners" and are afraid that their accent may get in the way and make it much harder for their counterpart to understand them. In fact, "managing" their accent so that it doesn't interfere is a legitimate concern—and a problem that shouldn't be underestimated. Spotty cellular coverage, frequent dropped calls, poor acoustics, and the lack of face-to-face clues—all contribute to making it harder for foreigners to speak on the phone with ease (especially with cell phones). It can be a very frustrating experience and more time-consuming than it should be. We know quite a few international executives who postpone a call indefinitely—or don't take a call—for fear they may not sound articulate and smart. Even if they take the time to jot down an outline of the points they want to cover, mentally rehearsing the conversation, they still dial the number with trepidation, especially if they are joining a conference call with multiple participants.

In short, phone interactions can be a source of serious anxiety for foreign-born professionals. We are frequently asked by our clients to help them be productive, pleasant and "natural" on the phone. And the reality is that, the more "natural" you want to sound, the more preparation you actually need.

Following are three types of phone situations, which present their own sets of challenges for international professionals: phone calls, voice mail, and conference calls.

Phone Calls

Even a simple phone call (i.e., not a complex conference call involving three time zones and several participants of different nationalities) can go wrong if you are not clear on what you want to accomplish. Don't let yourself be fooled by how casual a simple, old-fashioned phone call can seem. Business is still business.

People in the U.S. generally don't like to waste time on the phone. When you do pick up the phone, you need to be clear about your goal and your message. Keep the call short and to the point. Keep formalities and small talk to a minimum. State the reason for your call up front. End the call with a specific request, agreement, or offer.

Preparing a script or an outline of the points you want to cover will help make sure you don't forget anything important. Being focused and "on topic" conveys the impression of being serious about the call and being sensitive about the other person's time.

For those of you who are really nervous about talking on the phone, take heart: you may not have to force yourself after all! In fact, e-mail has taken over as the preferred form of communication in the U.S. It is not unusual for someone to e-mail a colleague who is sitting in another cubicle down the hall or in an office just a few feet away.

Voice Mail

Voice mail is a work tool and people use it more frequently than you might be accustomed to in your country. Americans don't really like to interrupt a meeting to answer the phone (and neither should you), therefore you will leave—and receive—many, many voice mail messages during a workday or even after hours.

You cannot underestimate the importance of leaving a well-crafted voice mail, as many business decisions are actually made via voice mail. While other parts of the world still rely on direct interactions to discuss sensitive topics, voice mail is an integral part of doing business in the U.S.: making decisions, placing orders, closing deals, etc. To underscore its importance, let's just mention that an international consulting firm runs a training program for its young associates just on how to leave a good voice mail!

The same rules of brevity and clarity apply to voice mail messages as they do to calls in general. There is nothing more irritating than a rambling, confusing message. It will be deleted instantly.

So, how do you leave a voice mail message that will be returned and acted upon?

- Specify the purpose of your call at the beginning.

- Be concise and to the point. If you can't be brief, clarify right away that this will be a long message so people can listen to it when they have time.

- Close by repeating what you want to have happen.

- Speak carefully, using all the sounds in the words, so your message can be understood.

The ability to leave good voice mail messages is like developing a muscle: with some practice you can train yourself to avoid situations like the following one:

A female Chinese executive left a voice mail to all the participants in a meeting the following day. To her amazement, nobody brought the materials she had mentioned in her voice mail. The reason? Her message was not understandable because of her accent and her convoluted instructions. The participants had not realized (or not understood) they were supposed to bring anything.

Conference Calls

In the U.S., conference calls are considered real meetings. In fact, because of the distances and different time zones people work in, there tend to be fewer in-person meetings and conference calls often replace face-to-face meetings. They are not just a way of keeping in touch or getting a quick update. They are virtual meetings—and that is the fundamental difference between a conference call in the U.S. versus one in other parts of the world.

Since conference calls are ubiquitous—it's common to have three or more conference calls a day—they have to be as productive as real meetings would be.

What do you need to do in order to ensure the success of a conference call in the U.S.? The same planning that goes into a meeting should go into a conference call.

Actually, even more planning is required because you are dealing with a large amount of logistical factors: time differences, acoustics, cell phone limitations, and the inability to see people's reactions, i.e., their body language.

Planning

Start your planning with the following considerations, as they will help define the call's agenda:

- *Why* are you organizing this call?
- What's the *result* you want to have?
- Is it achievable? If not, think of a *goal* you can reach.
- Who is instrumental in achieving this goal? Draw up a list of *participants*.
- What do participants need to know in order to achieve your objective? Determine the *materials* that need to be circulated ahead of time.
- What *topics* do you need to cover? What's the best sequence?

If you have answers to all these questions, you will have a rough idea of your call's agenda. But before you start writing it down, don't forget a series of standard steps that have become routine in the U.S. when organizing a conference call:

- Notifying all participants by e-mail well ahead of time;
- Circulating the initial agenda and incorporating any feedback;
- Getting the participants' agreement on the desired outcome;
- Sending out all the necessary pre-reading materials;
- Spelling out all the logistics, such as time (watch for different time zones), anticipated length of call, and call-in number; and
- Appointing a facilitator, a timekeeper, and a note-taker (if necessary).

These pre-call, preplanning steps are very important for several reasons: first, they help you set up a productive call; second, they help ensure that your colleagues view you as being in charge of the call. Acting as the leader of the call makes you more visible and can make your success more likely.

CONFERENCE CALL PLANNING CHECKLIST

☐ Desired outcome of call

☐ List of participants

☐ Materials needed

☐ Agenda

☐ Wrap-up process

Conducting a Conference Call

You need to take an active role in conducting the call if you want to be in charge of the call dynamics and ensure the call's result.

Your role should be evident from the beginning of the call.

We recommend sticking to the following tried and true approach that may seem a bit overstructured, but will work for sure.

- Start by introducing yourself and letting everybody else introduce him/herself.

- Name a facilitator, a timekeeper, and a note-taker (if necessary).

- Remind everybody of the time limits, the goal of the call, and the agenda.

- Verify that everybody is on the same page [in agreement].

- Start with the first point, and ask for contributions from the participants.

- Before moving on to the next point, summarize what has been decided, resolved, or left unresolved.

- Specify how you will deal with unresolved issues (If you skip this step, you will leave the impression that the call was a waste of time as certain issues will not be resolved).

- Constantly enforce time limits, e.g., "In the interest of time..."

- Constantly check for progress, e.g., "Is everybody OK with moving on to the next topic?"

- Don't interrupt (very tricky for some foreigners!), and make sure everyone has a chance to speak.

- Don't tune out to check your BlackBerry.

- Try to cover all the topics on the agenda. If you can't, agree on a process to reschedule the discussion.

- Specify next steps. Decide who is responsible for sending out meeting notes (or a relevant summary) and for following up on unresolved issues.

- Thank everybody for participating and mention when you will reconvene [meet or talk again].

Following Up

Send out meeting notes summarizing the highlights of the call, and make sure that participants follow up on their assigned tasks.

Typical Pitfalls: What Can Go Wrong

Language. Speaking clearly is very important. Because of the phone acoustics that may distort your words (and accentuate your accent), make it a point to speak clearly and enunciate well. Exaggerate the consonants in the words.

Don't be afraid to ask the participants to *avoid jargon* so that any non-native English speakers will have an easier time following the discussion.

Get to the point quickly. Being long-winded or verbose will just make it harder for others to follow you.

Be mindful of people's reactions. Judge the tone of voice they are using and the kinds of words they use—hesitant or convincing—and adjust your own. If you are in doubt, ask how they feel about the items discussed.

Be diplomatic. Keep in mind that disagreement is always better expressed in nuanced terms. So if you want to voice a negative opinion, it is safer to use expressions like: "It seems to me... I have the impression... please let me know if I am wrong..."

Remember that when delivering a controversial opinion or negative feedback, *positive comments always come first*, then any criticism. And that criticism is best made in private. For more on this topic, please see Chapter 9.

Logistics. Driving while taking a conference call is not a good option. It is not only a matter of safety: it is hard to concentrate on difficult topics while driving (and holding a cell phone at the steering wheel may be illegal). You should really make an effort to be in your office or in a location where you can focus on the discussion.

It is often easier to talk on a landline [office phone] rather than on a cell phone because acoustics are often difficult and coverage spotty with the latter.

Different time zones are often a difficult factor to manage, especially when Europe has started or ended Day Light Savings Time and the U.S. has not (typically, in the spring and fall).

Always double-check the time difference before you schedule a conference call.

Handling verbose participants. If one of the team members seems to be talking all the time and does not let others get their points across, it is really important that you or the facilitator step in fast and say something like: "These are excellent points you're making, but I would like to hear from people who haven't talked yet."

Handling shy or silent participants. If there are team members who don't say much during the call, you need to find out why. Is it because they are from a different culture and are not used to speaking out? Is there a difference of opinion?

Whatever it is, you can keep on asking for their opinion directly and eventually participants will feel encouraged to contribute. If at the end of a call, they have not really said much, it is advisable to talk with them in private after the call and find out what is going on.

Dealing with disagreement. If two or more people start arguing about an issue and can't resolve it quickly, you can suggest the issue should be discussed off-line [after the conference call] when more information is available.

Or you can do a process check and say, "In the interest of time..." or, "Let's get on with the agenda."

CONFERENCE CALL CHECKLIST

Before the call

☐ Invite participants via e-mail

☐ Specify all logistics (including dial-in number and code)

☐ Prepare the agenda, and send it to all participants

☐ Send out pre-reading materials

☐ Answer any questions pertaining to the call

During the call

☐ Make sure people entering the call introduce themselves

☐ Review the agenda

☐ Specify length of call

☐ Clarify expected outcome

☐ Assign various roles: facilitator, timekeeper, note-taker

☐ Make sure you know what your own role is in the call

☐ Reach closure on a topic before moving to the next one

☐ Summarize the main decisions reached and specify open issues

☐ At the end of the call, specify next steps follow-up items

☐ Don't check your BlackBerry

After the call

☐ Send out meeting notes summarizing the call

USEFUL TIPS FOR PHONE AND CONFERENCE CALLS

Helpful
Being mentally prepared even for simple phone calls
Keeping calls short and to the point
Leaving concise voice mail messages
Speaking clearly—managing your accent
Watching out for subtle clues of disagreement, e.g., silence, hesitant participation
Harmful
Wasting time on too many pleasantries
Not having a clear request/reason for the call
Neglecting the logistics of conference calls
Freezing in panic

6 How to Use E-Mail Effectively

Xavier was a budding football enthusiast who, during the football season, would often e-mail his buddies to get updates on the scores of his favorite teams. He did this during work hours and spent quite an amount of time online, discussing various aspects of the games. In addition, he would slip in some not so nice remarks abut his coworkers.

He was very surprised when he was called into his boss's office and officially reprimanded for having wasted so much company time when he was supposed to be working. Xavier had not known that his online actions would be monitored and recorded, and his chances for promotion were certainly diminished due to his excessive personal use of e-mail.

E-mail has become the main form of communication in the U.S. business world. It is not unusual for somebody to e-mail his/her colleagues down the hallway instead of picking up the phone or walking over to their office or cubicle.

As *MarketWatch* reports, "Everybody understands that now e-mail is not just the main communications medium, it's also a de facto filing system... it's standard evidence in litigation... That means workers need to consider the possibility of their e-mail going public."[15]

And, according to data reported in *Information Week*,[16] people get an average of 171 e-mail messages a day, and this number is expected to double by 2010. E-mail is not used just to share information—it is a communication as well as a management tool.

On the one hand, e-mail is ubiquitous and can never be really erased. On the other hand, we all know that many e-mails end up in the trash bin right away or are left unopened. So how do you make sure your e-mail messages are appropriate and are read by the recipient?

This chapter will address the elements that make e-mail messages effective and—most important—acted upon.

One short comment to our European readers: e-mail is referred to as "e-mail," not as "mail."

Mail is delivered by the mailman and does not come via computer, so if you are not clear with your word choice, you will confuse your colleagues.

Corporate E-Mail Policies

Before you even start using e-mail at your office, make sure you are familiar with your company's e-mail policy. Every company has one, and it is typically a template of common sense dos and don'ts. According to *MarketWatch*, "In some cases, those policies govern how much time workers can spend on personal e-mail each day, while other policies aim to restrict the people with whom the workers can interact by e-mail."

---

15. Coomes, Andrea. "Like Electronic DNA Evidence," MarketWatch, July 30, 2007.
16. Information Week, January 22, 2007.

While most companies don't mind the occasional use of e-mail for personal reasons, most will not tolerate *excessive personal use* of what is considered a work tool. In fact, most companies do monitor their employees' use of e-mail for both personal and business purposes, as they have the right to do so. Unlike some other countries where strict privacy protection laws shield the employee from company surveillance efforts, the U.S. has permissive laws that govern the right of companies to read and act on individual e-mails. "32% of firms say they employ staff to read or analyze outbound e-mail, and 17% said they employ someone whose 'primary or exclusive job function is to read or monitor e-mail...'"[17]

It's wise to establish a personal account for your private use outside of the office. Using e-mail inappropriately can get you into serious trouble in the U.S., certainly more so than in other cultures.

Anything you write can and often will be checked by IT, your bosses and supervisors; even if you delete the e-mail from the trash and from the "sent items," it is still on the server and it can be retrieved and read.

Don't write anything you would not want to see on the front page of the newspaper or that you would not want your boss to read. Information can easily leak when a message is forwarded to somebody outside the company, and it may end up in the hands of an overzealous reporter.

It seems that every month there is a new case in the paper about sensitive information that was leaked, e.g., a memo by the CEO, salary information, customer interviews—and most of these leaks are not malicious in nature. It all starts with a simple, naïve click.

U.S. E-Mail Habits

Especially in the Bay Area, people check their e-mail continuously. They are hooked on their PDAs, BlackBerrys or Treos. Their dependence on such devices has led to the expression "Crackberry," a play on words that refers to the dangerous BlackBerry addiction and the addictive drug known as crack.

---

17. MarketWatch, see above.

Many executives are in the habit of responding to e-mails immediately for fear of being overwhelmed by the sheer number of messages if they wait even half a day, or because they have adopted a stringent 24/7 mentality. Jokes on their "BlackBerry thumb" abound.

Like it or not, you are also expected to respond promptly to the messages you receive. It often doesn't matter if it's the weekend or a holiday—leaving the message unanswered in your inbox is an indication that either the message or the sender is not important for you.

Deciding on the Content of Your E-Mail

Greetings

In the U.S., most of the times you don't have to use formal titles, i.e., Dr. or Mr./Mrs. or Sir, in your greeting. As a matter of fact, most people just start the message with a simple "Hi," or use the first name, "John..." However, if you are writing to the CEO of the company or a higher official and you don't know them, it is appropriate to use their last names.

Body

Good e-mail messages are short, well-organized, and to the point.

Have only one or two clear objectives per e-mail. The goal of an e-mail is not to pour all of your ideas and suggestions into one e-mail, but rather to explain one or two clear points that you want to address.

Think twice before talking about sensitive topics via e-mail. When your e-mail addresses a delicate topic or when you need to generate consensus, nothing can replace a face-to-face exchange.

Don't write anything really negative. You never know—maybe the receiver of the e-mail is going to forward your e-mail to somebody else.

Double-check the content before sending. Most of the times, if you reread your e-mail before sending it out, you will notice you left out something or your ideas were not expressed clearly. You don't have to spend a huge amount of time, just reread—every time!—what you have written. You will be amazed at how many errors you'll still find.

Make the subject line explicit. Don't just send the e-mail back and forth with the same subject line—RE: re: re: re:. You need to have a subject line that really tells the recipient what the e-mail is about.

Bad subject line: "Meeting tomorrow"

Good subject line: "Meeting lunch room 5pm tomorrow re new budget 2008"

This way the reader, who may have twenty other meetings the next day (see Chapter 3), will know what the meeting is about and can prepare for it. Be as specific as you can be, for example, by including the time and location of the meeting, as this will make it hard for the participants to miss it.

A client of ours, a corporate coach who had just signed a new contract at a high-tech company, received an e-mail from HR with the title "Training." The e-mail listed the date and time for a training session for Group 1. Later the same day, she received another e-mail with the same title, "Training." She thought it was the same message and didn't open it, so she missed the details for the training session for Group 2. As a result, she came an hour late for the first meeting with her clients. The problem could have been easily avoided if the title had been more precise.

A good way to write effective subject lines is to think of them as newspaper headlines—you need to be brief and yet say enough to inform the readers about the content of the e-mail and entice them to read on.

Don't use e-mail as a way of "passing the buck" [avoiding responsibility]. You might think you have delegated your responsibility to someone else when you forward an e-mail in hopes of passing on the problem. But your colleagues will not appreciate this, and you will still be responsible for an action not taken.

Have a clear call to action at the end. If you want your e-mail to be useful, make sure you tell your readers what you want them to do. For example, if you want someone to get back to you at a specific date, include that at the end of the e-mail.

Closing

Don't expect a lot of formalities. A simple "Best Regards" will do; or if you know the recipients a bit better, you can say "Cordially" or "Cheers." Often, a "Thank You" is a good way to close.

Style

Brief is Best

Bullet points work really well; nowadays, people who receive e-mails with too much straight text will simply not read them.

Make Paragraph Breaks

Rather than having one large block of text, make (many) paragraph breaks between ideas, so that it is easier to digest the information (and include the bullet points).

Check Spelling

Spelling errors don't reflect well on you. Run a simple spellcheck every time before hitting the "send" button.

Use Polite Language

Whenever you have finished writing the e-mail and you are checking for content, grammar and spelling, try to insert a "please" and "thank you" wherever appropriate. This is always appreciated, especially when you e-mail colleagues from other cultures who put a great deal of importance on polite forms of writing.

Don'ts

Don't cc everyone you think might, should or could use the information.

Again, less is more. Send your information only to those people who need to see it.

Don't forward messages with a quick FYI at the beginning. The FYI might save you time, but it makes it harder for the recipients to figure out why they received the message. Always explain why you are forwarding it.

Don't send attachments (especially large attachments) unless they are expected or people know what they contain. No one wants a virus and many people won't open them.

Don't pass on jokes or funny sayings. Not everyone will appreciate or understand the humor and we all get enough spam. And do remember, "Big Brother" is always watching.

Don't send out your e-mail immediately. If you think you have to write something unpleasant (to someone on a virtual, global team, for example, whom you can't see in person), write it and then let it sit for a while. Often you'll realize that it might be too harsh or unclear, and it could easily be misinterpreted. It might be easier to pick up the phone.

Don't fall into the BlackBerry trap. Sometimes it's important to respond to messages right away. But most of the time, it is better to wait and craft a thoughtful response. Especially when you receive a message with content that you think is offensive, try not to react right away. It's easy to regret a hasty response.

Don't abuse group e-mailing lists. Check who is included and whether they all need to receive your message; if not, it might be preferable to address it to a smaller group.

Don't spam people. That means, don't put people on your e-mail list or newsletter list without first checking with them or without them sub-scribing. Always offer an easy option to unsubscribe. Take a look at the answer (verbatim) one of the authors received after asking that her name be removed from a mailing list: "Hi, you really want me to? I advise, if I may, that you change your message to something like 'I appreciate your gesture of including me in your list but would rather pass this opportunity as my inbox is full and overwhelming. If you want me to read your material, kindly wait until I can do so'...." Clearly, this was written by a foreign professional who was not aware of e-mail etiquette in the United States and was lecturing inappropriately.

> **ELEMENTS OF EFFECTIVE E-MAILS**
> ☐ A clear subject line
> ☐ Objective
> ☐ State the problem
> ☐ Suggest the solution
> ☐ Call to action

Exercise

Take a look at the following e-mail sent to a Bay Area lawyer by a European colleague.

Dear Dr. Smith,

Thank you very much for writing to me. I appreciated so much hearing from you. The reason I am writing this e-mail to you is that the document you sent me was incomplete. Some of the sections were very difficult to decipher, and there were also typing errors. That way, it took me a long time to read and understand it.

I am afraid that if I rewrite it, it will take me at least half a day and currently I do not have the time for this kind of project. I think that I will see you in a month at the conference and I am hoping we can talk about it then in person.

Rewrite the message in a more positive way.

Here is a possible, more polite rewrite.

Dear Dr. Smith,

Thank you very much for your e-mail. I appreciated receiving the document. Unfortunately, I wasn't quite sure what you wanted me to do with it. Would you mind taking a few minutes to review the materials for accuracy and typos, and let me know how to proceed? Perhaps we could discuss this at the upcoming conference.

USEFUL TIPS FOR USING E-MAIL EFFECTIVELY

Helpful
Writing short e-mails, and to the point
Checking every message for clarity and typos, twice
Having a clear request at the end
Using simple language
Responding promptly
Harmful
Ignoring your company's e-mail policy
Being long-winded
Sending large files that clog the recipient's e-mail box
Sending unnecessary e-mails to everyone
Abusing e-mail, e.g., passing on responsibility

7 How to Conduct Successful Job Interviews in the U.S.

José Louis, a Brazilian university graduate, steps tentatively into the office of the department manager. He stands deferentially until she invites him to take a seat. The conversation starts on a very formal tone. When the manager asks him to describe his background, they discover they attended the same university. They share fond memories of a literature course, and José Louis mixes a couple of literary quotations into the conversation in hopes of impressing the interviewer. She is indeed impressed by his erudition, as they keep debating the merits of Thoreau's Walden.

After about an hour, the manager announces she has another meeting coming up, and asks him to go into more details about his job experience. He describes the internship he did as part of his Master's Degree program and mentions the many useful connections he made there. He also indicates that his family is very supportive of his move to this new, potential employer. They agree he could be a good fit for the company and immediately make another appointment to continue the dialogue. The manager is late to her next meeting, but she is happy as she senses he is probably the right candidate. José Louis also thinks that it was a very good first meeting: it ran over by half an hour!

Switch to the San Francisco Bay Area, same company, same position.

Janet strides confidently across the room to shake the interviewer's hand. She starts the conversation by stating how excited she is about this opportunity. When the department manager asks her to describe her background, she gives a quick overview of her qualifications and relevant job experience. She details how a couple of volunteer projects she has been responsible for have sharpened her skills necessary for this position. She asks a few thoughtful questions about the company which show that she has done quite a bit of research already. After about an hour the interview is over. Both feel good about how it went, and the manager tells Janet (calling her by her first name) that HR will be in touch with her soon.

José Louis' style reflects the more relaxed interviewing practices common in South America, but his style wouldn't necessarily play well in the U.S. Janet, by contrast, is right at home with U.S. practices.

When interviewing for U.S. jobs, international candidates are as qualified and as competent as American candidates are, but they don't always come across as confident. As a result, they frequently don't get the job or they have to go through a longer process to get it. Why?

Even if you sound like a native speaker of English, cross-cultural differences can get in the way of a successful interview for you. The words you use, the skills you choose to emphasize—or the ones you leave out—all may contribute to a credibility gap.

The differences can be really subtle: unusual word choices, different sentence structure, examples, and anecdotes. All of these unconscious choices add up to create an impression of you as a solid candidate, but perhaps not the best one. They feed a common misperception of foreign candidates being perfectly qualified from a professional standpoint, but somehow lacking the personal characteristics necessary to succeed in a particular job.

In essence, how you look and how you sound may end up undermining your chances.

What can you do differently?

The Right Mindset

Understand that interviews in the U.S. are an opportunity for you to explicitly sell your skills. This may feel awkward to you—as it does to most foreigners—but there is no escaping the game: in an interview, you have to sell your skills, your talents, and your expertise. Of course, you have to do it graciously and ethically, but you can't underestimate the importance of acquiring—even just temporarily—the right mindset to do this well.

Presenting yourself in the best possible light is something that is ingrained in most Americans through the U.S. educational system, which tends to emphasize personal achievement and individual success from the early grades on. Even in kindergarten, children are encouraged to talk about their experiences and share them with their classmates in a positive, optimistic way.

Many foreign students are uncomfortable with the idea of shining under the spotlight and, as a result, they never master the art of tooting their own horn [singing their own praises] for the purpose of standing out, smoothly, genuinely, and naturally. Regardless of whether you came here as a student or later in life, if you don't make the effort to differentiate yourself as a candidate and present yourself in the best light possible, you won't go very far.

You need to get comfortable with the idea of scrutinizing your track record [academic, professional, and personal resume], selecting your most distinctive accomplishments, and then deliberately emphasizing them during the interview.

So get into the right frame of mind. Practice self-promotion. Turn your CV (curriculum vitae) into a marketing tool. It is not only acceptable—it is essential.

In fact, the curriculum vitae—a detailed list of all your qualifications and work experiences—is not a very useful tool in the U.S. A resume is a preferable option: a single-page overview of your skills and accomplishments that shows your fit for a specific job.[18]

Promoting Yourself with Honesty and Integrity

Self-promotion [representing yourself well] goes hand in hand with honesty and integrity. You cannot misrepresent yourself. You cannot, and should not, inflate or "invent" your qualifications. Too many executives have been fired or forced to resign once the company they were working for found out they doctored their CVs (e.g., the CEO of Radio Shack in 2006; the Dean of Admissions at MIT in 2007).

However, we find that most foreigners tend to make the opposite mistake and present their accomplishments in a very understated way. This approach won't work either. Make sure you list all your qualifications and accomplishments matter-of-factly on your resume. And, try to weave them into the conversation casually and frequently during a personal interview.

Since many American employers may not be familiar with your country's educational system, take the time to explain how well regarded the school you attended is, perhaps by mentioning comparable U.S. institutions.

Offering Meaningful Examples and Anecdotes

Just like a picture is worth a thousand words, anecdotes are a way to illustrate your point effectively.

---

18. For more details on the difference between CVs and resumes, please see The International MBA Student's Guide to the U.S. Job Search. San Francisco: Wet Feet Press, 2006, page 64.

Offering insightful examples and anecdotes and interesting stories is a must in order to lend credibility to your statements about yourself. So, be sure you prepare a good number of real-life examples about your personal and professional life.

How can you turn your previous experiences into memorable stories that set you apart from other candidates?

First rule: keep it *short*. Prepare your examples and stories ahead of time and make sure they are focused and well organized. Don't ramble around looking for the point of the story (the actual point you want to make). Stick to a formula that always works: problem, resolution, result.

For example: "I once had to spearhead a team of executives negotiating with a supplier who was not willing to give us a break [reduce the price] on prices at all. I proposed a compromise on volume and managed to get a three percent price reduction."

Second: keep it *relevant*. Use only examples, brands, and names that your American interviewer is familiar with and can relate to. So, instead of saying "I was a branch director at Banco Santander in Valencia," say "I was a VP at a major regional bank, the Spanish equivalent of Citigroup, with oversight for the entire region."

Third: make it *tangible*. Quantify the results you have achieved through a particular experience. This helps make sure your interviewer has a real appreciation for your accomplishment. Americans love numbers. While a Frenchman might say, "I was responsible for introducing the new reporting system," an American candidate would phrase the same concept as, "I reorganized the sales reporting system and boosted revenues by five percent."

Make sure you prepare and practice at least three anecdotes that illustrate your strengths. And don't forget that you will probably also need a couple of stories about your weaknesses; focus on how your weaknesses or failures worked out as learning experiences. Failure is acceptable in the U.S., as long as you learn from it and recover. Therefore, instead of admitting failure point blank by saying: "I was not able to convince my boss to introduce product X on the market," try something like: "I learned that in order to persuade a superior to introduce a new product, I had to build a coalition of supporters who could influence his/her decision."

Honing Your Pitch

Your pitch is a brief overview statement about yourself as a professional.

A personal pitch is also called a headline message because, just as a good newspaper headline captures the essence of a given piece and helps sell papers, the pitch helps convey what makes you distinctive.

In a future-oriented culture like the American one, your pitch is a forward-looking statement that summarizes your aspirations *and* how your qualifications will lead you forward.

Most people think that "your pitch" is all about your previous experiences and qualifications. So they tend to craft a pitch that emphasizes their past accomplishments. But a good pitch is actually more about your future than it is about your past. It tells the interviewer who you are and who you want to become.

Take a look at the popular formula below for help in crafting your pitch:

your past experience + your unique qualities and skills
+ your passion and motivation = a good pitch

For example:

"I am a software engineer with a passion for product development," instead of "I have ten years of experience in software development."

Or: "I am an accent reduction specialist who loves to help foreign professionals improve their communication skills," instead of "I am an accent reduction specialist with 10 years of experience working with foreign-born professionals."

It's not as easy as it sounds. The passion component is just as important as the experience. This typically seems awkward to international professionals, who are more used to describing their degrees and years of experience rather than dwelling on their real passion in life. But in the U.S., where the boundaries between personal and professional life are often blurry, talking about your aspirations and about what motivates you in your professional life (i.e., in your life in general) is not only the norm—it is expected.

Exercise: Let's work on your own pitch.

Take a piece of paper and craft a twenty-word statement about yourself that captures the essence of your experience, skills, and passion. Read it out loud.

How does it sound? If it takes longer than a minute to read it, go back and shorten it, without leaving anything important out. Try again.

Speaking English Like a Native (or Almost)

Most international professionals tend to replicate in English the stylistic choices they make in their native language. So they use a lot of nouns and few verbs. They tend to use complex, long-winded sentence structures—with several subordinate clauses introduced by but, which, etc.—because for them, it sounds educated. For example, a foreign-born professional might say: "After several quarters of declining sales due to the company's inability to develop leading edge products, there was an increase in sales of twenty percent following our team's efforts to introduce more advanced features."

Listen to how an American candidate would have phrased the same concept: "I increased sales by twenty percent by introducing innovative products." That's the difference between nouns and verbs, and passive versus active sentence structure.

American English places a premium on simplicity so, whenever you can, use a verb instead of a noun and use an active sentence structure instead of a passive one. Chances are, this will not only help you speak correctly but will also make you sound much more like an American (for more on language choices, see Chapter 9).

Another mistake international professionals frequently make is using too many qualifiers. A typical sentence we hear when coaching our clients on job interviews goes like this: "I *believe* I *would be* able to contribute my significant experience to your company." Instead, try the following: "I *will* contribute my five years of direct experience."

As a foreign-born professional, you will probably err on the side of saying "we" instead of "I" fairly frequently; yet, the American culture favors individual initiative and accomplishments, so go ahead and say: "I did it, I got the contract signed." even if this might sound arrogant to you. Unless you massively overdo it, what sounds arrogant to you will only sound self-confident to your audience. Being modest and humble won't get you anywhere in an interview (in the U.S.).

Your accent may also get in the way, so be sure to practice your lines well enough in order to minimize any accent or intonation. The best thing is to work on your accent (perhaps by getting accent reduction training) well ahead of your interviews, since it takes time to change bad language habits and relearn word intonations. Americans (as well as most other monolingual people), have a hard time understanding words that don't sound anything like they are supposed to (unless they are in frequent contact with foreign professionals, as on the East and West coasts). And they will be too polite to tell you that they had no clue [didn't understand] what you said; so you can leave the interview convinced that you did really well, only to find out later that you won't be called back. Why? Simply because the interviewer couldn't get a complete picture of you due to your language "handicap."

Exercise: Analyze Your Style

Practice an interview with a friend. Try out your pitch. Make an effort to use the right vocabulary and anecdotes. Record his/her feedback on the chart below. Then try again.

STYLE ANALYSIS

What works	What doesn't work
Vocabulary	
Attitude	

Doing Your Research

American companies expect candidates to do their research and to come to the interview with a good understanding of the potential employer. In general, the more you know about a company, the better prepared you are to engage in a meaningful dialogue. This will show you are serious about a job, and it will also allow you to turn the interview into a two-way information exchange. You are getting information out of the interviewer as much as he or she is getting insights into your abilities. An interview is rarely just a one-way exchange in the U.S. You are not only entitled to take on a more active role by asking questions yourself, you are actually expected to do so. Particularly well received are questions that show your understanding of the company or the position. Such a proactive approach is highly appreciated and valued.

There are plenty of resources available online to use for your research, including the official company Web site, industry newsletters and organizations, the competitors' Web sites, and media outlets. And don't forget that networking can be a good way to gather some nuggets [pieces of gold] of information that are not publicly available. Should your interviewer have written a book or white paper, reading them ahead of time and weaving them into the conversation will set you apart from other candidates.

Looking Good

Psychologists say that as much as fifty percent of a hiring decision is made within the first sixty seconds. Personal appearance does matter. Even though it sounds obvious, candidates need to make a conscious effort to *look* very professional—and so many do not, unfortunately.

If you are going after a professional or managerial role in corporate America, as a rule, you need to present a well-groomed, clean, fairly conservative image. In this case, it's best to err on the side of blending in, i.e., of looking as most people do within a certain industry or company. So if you are interviewing at a law firm or a well-established corporation, go with the traditional business attire (typically, though not uniquely, a suit for both men and women) and for men, a clean, shaven look.

If you are applying for a job at a hip creative agency or a young high-tech company that prides itself on going against the rules, a more casual look might be appreciated—so wearing clean jeans and a sweatshirt (for men) with the logo of a selective university (which you hopefully attended) is perfectly appropriate, especially if you apply as a engineer (and it's dress-down Friday). For women, a nice pair of pants or a skirt (nothing too provocative) with a quality T-shirt and a jacket is also OK.

When in doubt, find out what others at the company wear, and go for the same look.

In any case, respect the American rule of personal hygiene (i.e., frequent showering and therefore no personal odors), make sure your hair is nicely trimmed, don't show off any tattoos or body piercing; for women, keep the perfume and jewelry to a bare minimum.

Body Language

Body language is crucial in conveying your interest in the job, and therefore it plays a major role in creating the right impression.

Most interviews start with a handshake, which should be firm; in the U.S., a weak handshake will reflect poorly on you as it is considered a sign of being unreliable. This is something that you can practice with your American colleagues. If you are too shy to ask them to assess your handshake, just watch and see how they do it when they shake your hand. But don't underestimate its importance in Western culture.

Your posture also sends a signal: if you are sitting, make sure your back is straight and your body is slightly leaning forward, which conveys an attitude of interest. A client of ours was very confident about an interview but she didn't get the job offer. When she went back to check what happened (an excellent way of finding out what went wrong and to learn what to avoid in the future), the interviewer told her that she was so casual in her posture, sitting back lazily in the chair, they were convinced she didn't really want the job.

We've also worked with clients from Asia who sat with a rounded back, hands between their knees, leaning forward. This can be an acceptable way of showing respect in some Asian countries, but in the U.S., it makes people look insecure and subservient.

Your gestures should be natural, mostly limited to the upper part of your body (the interviewer will only see your upper body anyway, if you are sitting). If you can, observe your interviewer's body language and gestures and adapt your own to them; this is called mirroring, and it's based on the belief that we all tend to like people who look like us. People with more conservative movements do not appreciate having hands waved in front of their faces, so be careful of your hand movements while talking.

Maintain eye contact with the interviewer throughout the conversation. While in some cultures looking down and not directly at a superior is a sign of respect, that is not the case in the U.S. A lack of eye contact sends a subliminal message of being shifty.

Nodding in agreement and other facial clues of being engaged in the exchange are necessary, while just sitting there and listening—which is a more accepted behavior in Asian cultures—makes interviewers feel that you are indifferent to the substance of the conversation.

Last but not least, remember to smile frequently throughout the interview. Americans are a fundamentally optimistic people, and they value a positive attitude. Smiling will send a signal of friendliness and self-confidence, no matter how nervous and anxious you are.

Showing enthusiasm for the job also conveys a positive, can-do attitude, which will help make a good impression.

But, don't overdo it with body language. Especially if you come from a more physical culture (e.g., a South American or a Mediterranean country), it's easy to think that some kind of physical contact (e.g., a formal hug or a pat on the back) might be a good way to part at the end of a successful interview. Instead, a smile or a polite handshake works better in the U.S.

In general, remember to respect personal space (in the U.S., it's about 18 inches, or about 50 centimeters between people), so keep a comfortable distance. If you get too close, your interviewer will feel uncomfortable and might actually start backing up away from you to avoid the proximity.

Good Listening Skills

Interrupting someone while he or she is talking is never a good idea in the U.S. It may be perfectly acceptable in your home country or even a sign of a lively debate, but it is considered very rude here. So never, ever, ever interrupt the interviewer—unless you want to make a lasting *negative* impression.

What are the signs of good listening?

Appearing engaged, nodding in agreement, maintaining eye contact, asking probing questions during a pause in the conversation or when the interviewer has completed a full sentence or a thought, rephrasing a statement to make sure you understood it properly, clarifying a point, inserting yourself politely by asking, "If I may interject here..."—all of these behaviors implicitly say, "I'm listening."

On one hand, not interrupting is hard for South Americans and Southern Europeans, where interrupting is a fact of life and no one thinks twice about doing it.

On the other hand, the American way of listening (being actively engaged) is also hard for Asian candidates, especially the Chinese, who tend to have a more deferential listening demeanor. Yet, passively waiting for your turn with a deferential attitude, and perhaps marking the transition with a couple of minutes of respectful silence, can easily be misinterpreted as a sign of indifference or, even worse, of an inability to really grasp the conversation. You have to give your interviewer some visual clues that you understand him or her: again, smile, nod, rephrase, clarify, etc.

Handling the Mechanics of the Actual Interview: Opening, Closing, and Next Steps

As you arrive at the company where the interview will take place, it is extremely important to be friendly and courteous with everybody, irrespective of status. From the receptionist on up, be nice, be polite, smile. Your actions may well be monitored when you least expect it. Call your counterpart by their title—Mrs., Mr., Doctor, or whatever is appropriate—unless they ask you to switch to first names.

When you meet the interviewer, use the first few minutes to establish a personal connection. Smile, look the other person in the eyes, and offer a pleasantly firm handshake. Take a minute to ask a personal question, to make a comment about something you have in common, or to remark on a photo on the interviewer's desk—family? Sports? Recent local news? Anything that can help break the ice.

Now would also be a good time to mention something that you have read in your research about the interviewer, for example: his/her university, something in the news, his/her move up in the company, etc. All of these points will show you are genuinely interested and did your homework!

At the end of the interview, don't forget to discuss the next steps. It is completely appropriate to ask about the process and timing for the hiring decision, i.e., when the final decision will be made and when can you expect to hear from the company.

For example, you can ask: "When may I count on hearing from you, and what else can I do to answer your questions?"

Discuss financial information only at the end (this topic typically comes up in the second round of interviews), and only if the interviewer asks. The standard advice is to be honest about your compensation level, while making sure you mention every line item that is included in your package (benefits, vacations, flex time...everything tangible and intangible).

Always follow up with a thank-you note a day or two after an interview. Try to summarize the key points discussed and offer additional perspectives or information you may not have had handy during the interview (but keep it short). An e-mail is perfectly acceptable and is the norm. If you want to stand out or you are dealing with a rather old-fashioned environment, write a personal, handwritten note on nice stationery—but make sure it is error-free.

Follow-up calls. If you haven't heard back from the company after a couple of weeks, it is a good idea to place a follow-up call to make sure they received your note and to check where things stand. Be careful not to seem too eager or impatient. In other words, call once, not several times. If you have a competing offer, specify that and wait for the company's reaction.

Preparing Your References

Make sure you have prepared your references ahead of time. That means making a list of the individuals who can vouch for you and who can attest to your skills and talents. Also make your references aware they might receive a call from your prospective employer. Be aware that your list is just a starting point for the recruiter, who will then start cross-checking your references with people who were not on you initial list.

Fielding Hostile Questions

Some interviewers just rejoice in being hostile. It may be a reflection of the company's culture, or it may be a deliberate technique to observe your behavior under stress. Your best bet is to defuse the questions, smile, and stay calm. Ask yourself if it is worth getting a job in a company that fosters a confrontational culture or condones a demeanor that is openly hostile.

TEN MOST FREQUENTLY ASKED QUESTIONS

1. Tell me about yourself.
2. Run me through your resume.
3. What are your main strengths and weaknesses?
4. What's your biggest accomplishment? What's your biggest failure?
5. What are your career goals in five years?
6. Why are you interested in this job/in our company?
7. Why should I hire you (and not someone else)?
8. What other opportunities are you looking at?
9. What has been your toughest professional situation?
10. Describe a situation in which you exercised a leadership role.

Handling Illegal Questions

Questions on the following topics are illegal in the U.S.: age, marital status, country of origin, religion, sexual orientation, health status, and criminal record. Interviewers cannot ask you any questions about these subjects. If you are asked any such questions, you are not obligated to answer. In fact, you have three choices: you can answer, you can state that you are aware that is an illegal question, or you can offer a diplomatic formula like: "I am not sure how that relates to the job, but I can assure you that it wouldn't pose a problem."

On the other hand, it is perfectly legal for the interviewer to ask you for proof of eligibility to work in the U.S., or whether you have ever been convicted of a crime as it relates to the job for which you are applying. For example, if you are applying for a job as a treasurer, the prospective employer can ask you if you have ever been convicted of embezzlement, but not if you have ever been convicted of drunk driving.

INTERVIEW PREPARATION CHECKLIST

☐ Research the industry

☐ Research the company

☐ Hone your pitch

☐ Prepare stories/anecdotes

☐ Prepare questions

☐ Practice, practice, practice

USEFUL TIPS FOR INTERVIEWING IN THE U.S.

Helpful

Being prepared, i.e., thinking through questions ahead of time

Being self-confident

Practicing the interview with a friend or professional coach

Researching the company ahead of time

Conveying enthusiasm

Turning the interview into a dialogue

Writing a personal thank you note

Following up

Harmful

Being too modest or too passive

Not having examples/anecdotes to support your points

Arriving late

Being vague

Interrupting

Talking about money in the first session

Neglecting to follow up

8 How to Hold Your Own with the U.S. Media

An Indian entrepreneur, the CEO of a Bay Area-based start-up that provides wireless services to global telecom companies, was keen on having his company profiled on the front page of the Wall Street Journal. Such an ambitious goal was obviously hard to achieve, and was actually not very meaningful for his company as it didn't reach the company's target audience. As expected, the WSJ rebuffed any attempt to schedule an interview. But The Financial Times showed some interest in the story, as the paper was gathering information for an article on innovative wireless services that it was planning to publish within a few weeks. The FT was actually a much better fit for this particular start-up, as some of the company's prospective clients were major European and Asian telecom companies.

An initial phone interview was scheduled and was to be followed by an in-person meeting. But a calendar conflict arose, and the phone interview slipped in the CEO's list of priorities. The CEO wound up calling the FT reporter on his cell phone from the airport in Mumbai, rushing to catch a flight, with about 12 hours of time difference and a spotty connection. The interview turned out hectic and unfocused. As a conse-

*quence, the in-person meeting never took place. There was no
mention of this entrepreneur, his company or its innovative services in
the article that eventually appeared in the FT.*

*The CEO first ignored his PR consultant's advice, then mismanaged a
unique opportunity, and never got the coverage he craved.*

*Later on, when the CEO was finally persuaded that it would be more
practical and more beneficial for the company to target industry publications, the company was profiled on a trade magazine popular with
telecom CTOs. Shortly afterwards, this start-up got a major contract
from a European Telecom company.*

A Snapshot of the U.S. Media Landscape

The U.S. media landscape is a very dispersed market, with a lot of
prestigious dailies and several well-respected local papers. There are
also numerous business publications as well as countless indus-
try-specific newsletters (such as Business 2.0, INC, and Entrepreneur)
Add a number of reputable business broadcast outlets (CNBC, CNN,
etc.) and popular Internet vehicles (online publications and blogs) to
the mix, and you get a pretty complex picture. No wonder it's hard for
international professionals to figure out how to navigate these treacherous waters!

Let's start by saying that, if your goal is to shape or protect your reputation in the U.S., you really have to get to know all the media outlets
available. You should read as much as you can in terms of national,
local, and industry press and regularly check out the most popular
Web-based publications for your line of business. Get an idea of what
topics they cover and their "angles," i.e., their points of view.

Because of the sheer size of the market, there is a great degree of spe-
cialization for reporters in the U.S., and therefore, you can expect the
reporter covering your beat to be quite knowledgeable about the
subject matter.

Speed to publication matters a lot in the U.S.—no reporter wants to be
out-scooped, i.e., beaten by a colleague with fresher news—so the
rhythms of interacting with a reporter can be quite frantic. But speed to

publication also means that reporters have less time for investigative journalism, so they are likely to apply a lesser degree of scrutiny to the information they receive because of time constraints.

E-mail is the preferred way of communicating with reporters. Most likely, the first contact with a reporter will happen via e-mail rather than by phone, as is more customary in Europe, for example.

Overall, the U.S. is a highly sophisticated media market where content carries more weight than a personal relationship with the individual reporter.

Media: Friend or Foe?

We have seen quite a few foreign executives get into serious trouble for misspeaking during an interview. Take the case of a San Fran-cisco-based venture capitalist, originally from Europe, who revealed to a reporter that he thought company X was doomed to failure. Even though this venture capitalist had indeed specified to the reporter that he was providing this information "off the record"—i.e., without being quoted by name—he wound up with his name in print anyway, probably because he didn't know he couldn't trust that specific reporter. The remark did not sit well with his partners, and he didn't make any friends in the process.

There are numerous courses and seminars specifically dedicated to the dos and don'ts of dealing with the media. Often, they are offered by local colleges or universities as part of their continuing education programs, as well as by private organizations such as the Public Relations Society of America (PRSA), or other PR companies/media training boutique firms.

If you think you will find yourself in front of a camera or will have to field a reporter's call fairly frequently, we strongly recommend taking one of these seminars. Better yet, if either you and/or your company have the resources, engage the services of a professional media trainer—you won't be sorry.

There is no denying that engaging with the media can be tricky. For example, you should be aware that any casual conversation with a reporter—even a friend of yours—at a cocktail party can wind up with your name and a quote in the newspaper the next morning—or worse, you can end up being misquoted. Even worse, a slip of the tongue [unintentional remark] can end up on Google or YouTube, which can haunt you for the rest of your professional life (as happened to some U.S. politicians). For example, a prospective employer "Googling" your name might come across an inappropriate quote of yours that wound up published in your university's paper months or years before.

Choose Your Approach

Especially if you are in a profession in which exposure to the media is part of the game (investment banking, venture capital, or new, "hot" technologies, to name a few), you might find yourself in the position of fielding an unsolicited reporter's call (or e-mail).

What do you do if a reporter calls for a comment on a topic that is within your area of expertise?

Or if you want to make a name for yourself as an expert in your field?

How should you proceed?

First, be aware of your company's policy for dealing with reporters. In most cases, companies have a specific protocol in place that requires you to refer the reporter's call to a spokesperson.

Then, you also need to ask yourself whether you stand to gain or lose by interacting with the media. The underlying question is: what's in it for you?

Reasons in favor of engaging actively with the media might include the following:

- You would like to make a career change and think that being mentioned in the media as an expert on a given topic will help.

- You would like to establish yourself as an authority in your field.

- You want to make a name for your new business.

- You have been asked to bolster your company's reputation.

- You want to set the record straight about a misunderstanding that directly affects your or your company's reputation.

But there are also good reasons in favor of staying out of the media spotlight; they might include the following:

- You don't have a clear message and/or don't know enough about the topic.

- The message you want to convey might be controversial.

- You could get fired or make enemies if you are misquoted.

- You don't stand to gain anything.

These are just a few examples. Just be clear about your reasons to engage or to not engage with the media.

So, if you think it's in your interest to start building a relationship with key reporters, do take the call (or reply to the e-mail) according to your company's guidelines and try to be as helpful as you can to that reporter. That way, in the future, he or she will see you as a reliable source of information.

But again, do you really want to see your name "in print"? If you don't have a good reason to take the call, you are probably better off declining politely. Just remember that, if you are going to decline the reporter's request for comment, you need to reply quickly and be re-spectful of the reporter's time and deadlines. That way you will stay on good terms.

If you do want to engage actively with the media, the approach you take depends on whether you are already well known to reporters or if you are starting from scratch trying to contact them.

If the media know you and view you as an interesting source of infor-mation, they will probably contact you directly. All you have to do is cultivate these relationships, by replying to their requests in a timely manner and, whenever possible, by offering to provide additional infor-mation. Be as helpful and as friendly as you can, and eventually you will become a trusted source and a reliable thought partner to the reporters who cover your beat [area of expertise]. This will ensure some degree of exposure for you.

But if you are the one trying to make the first contact with the media, here are some steps you can take:

First, make yourself useful to them and proactively reach out with valuable information. Start by becoming a frequent presence at industry forums, events and organizations that are of interest to journalists (check the event's Web site to determine media attendance). Participate in panels where you can share your expertise. Whether you are there as a participant or as a speaker, you can be spotted as an interesting contributor or as a source of information. It may take a few speeches or presentations for the reporters covering your area to take notice, but eventually they will. And you will be recognized as an expert in the field.

Second, identify the reporters covering your beat by monitoring what appears in all the relevant publications. Then approach them directly (mostly via e-mail) with either a personal message or a comment on a piece they have already published, offering to make yourself available for further information (this is also a good way to go if you can't make the necessary time investment to participate in industry events).

Don't start by targeting national business outlets (print or broadcast) such as the *Wall Street Journal* or *Business Week*, as they are much harder to reach. It's easier to start by approaching the following: local newspapers, trade or professional publications, industry newsletters, local radio or TV stations that cover business news, Internet media. Make sure you check their websites before contacting them, as many publications provide an editorial calendar of topics they plan to cover in the near future.

Preparing for the Interview

Once you have managed to make contact with a reporter and have agreed to an interview, there is a lot you can do to ensure it is a positive, productive experience for both of you.

Do Your Homework

Do you know the reporter? Let's assume that Liz Johnson of the Daily News contacts you. What is her reputation? Is she considered to be aggressive, or does she play a fair game? What can you learn from her previous stories? Does she have an agenda? Does she have any bias against you or your message?

What about the outlet (publication or TV show)? Is it typically associated with one side or the other of the debate? What type of audience does it reach? Is this audience relevant for your goals?

Agree on the Ground Rules

Decide whether you want to be interviewed "off the record," i.e., identified by profession and other characteristics, but not by your name; as a background source, i.e., without being identified; or for attribution, i.e., with your name next to a quote.

Reporters love quoting people by name, but generally, if you don't feel comfortable being associated with a certain statement, it's best to ask to be treated as a background source. If you agree to be quoted by name, you should ask to review and approve your quotes. Any good reporter will grant you this preview, although no reporter will agree to show you more than your quotes. That means that you still run the risk of being quoted out of context, which can lead to misinterpretations. That's why it's important to do your homework first and decide whether or not you can trust a reporter.

Hone Your Message—Speak in Sound Bites

Reporters and viewers/readers have no time and no patience for long-winded, rambling thoughts. Information in today's world must be distilled into clear, understandable messages: that means you have to train yourself to speak with quick sound bites, interesting headlines, and crisp snippets of information.

It takes practice, but it is doable for everybody. Here's how.

Start by writing down your core message, then say it out loud, edit and revise it—several times until you get it right. It has to be quick, clear, and concise. Try it out with friends and colleagues. Say it out loud several times so you are sure you can articulate it smoothly. We also advise our clients to prepare several versions of their core message, so they can get their point across repeatedly, without sounding like a broken record.

Honing your message is critical because, once you "have it down," you can bridge to it whenever you have a chance. You might laugh at all the preparation we recommend, but the easygoing executive you see out there talking smoothly about his company on TV has had many hours of training by a professional media trainer—that's why he sounds so good.

Example of a bad message: "The economy is expected by the company's executives to show a significant improvement in the third quarter."

A better version: "Management expects the economy to turn around by the end of the year."

Line Up Your Evidence

You'll need credible evidence to substantiate your core message. List all the facts, numbers, and statistics that can prove your point. Then select the ones that are most convincing and interesting, and train yourself to illustrate them concisely and clearly. This is very hard for foreign-born professionals, who are used to giving detailed explanations; that does not work here. Your evidence has to be short and pack some punch [have a sharp effect].

Whenever possible, choose anecdotes over figures. Remember that stories capture people's imagination much better than numbers, and it's stories that reporters are after.

Speak Clearly and Concisely

The easiest way to get your message across is to keep it short and simple.

The longer and more complex, the more likely it is that you will be misunderstood, misquoted, or not quoted at all.

Conciseness is particularly critical for broadcast interviews. A good way to keep it simple and brief is to boil down your information to three to five main points. Write them down—in bullet points—on an index card; make sure they fit on the index card to pass the conciseness test. You should be able to say each one of them in twenty seconds or less.

If you are concerned about accuracy, a good technique is to hand the reporter a background sheet (a press release, a brochure, a fact sheet, or some statistics) so he or she can check the facts and can choose to include more information in the article or segment.

Also, you can leave a one-page summary of your main points for accuracy, with your contact information where you can be reached for follow-up questions.

Anticipate Questions

Prepare the ten toughest questions you think you may be asked, and practice your answers. Not only will this prepare you to field the actual questions with ease, it will also boost your self-confidence, which will come across during the interview.

Bridge—Return to Your Main Point Often

Every time a reporter asks an open-ended question, take the opportunity to "bridge," i.e., to repeat your main point: briefly address the question and then transition to your core message. For example, let's assume your main message is that your company's profits have increased. You make this point explicitly early on during the interview. Later, when addressing a question on rising costs, you can take the opportunity to bridge back to your main message by saying something like: "Rising costs are always a concern, but we are encouraged by our increase in profits."

Manage Anxiety

It's very natural to feel nervous in front of a camera, and quite a few people end up forgetting their lines, especially when they are speaking in a foreign language. In addition, there are a lot of distractions during a typical interview that you may not have considered before: the noise or lights from a nearby studio where another segment is being recorded, the various cameras taping you from different angles, the interviewer checking different source feeds... a lot of things go on that may cause you to lose your focus. Don't panic. "Stage anxiety" is something most people learn to manage, and you can do that, too.

You may want to bring a few small cards with bullet points that help you remember your main message and your supporting evidence (facts and anecdotes). Be calm, take it slowly, smile, and your lines will all come back.

Check How You Look

The way you look and the confidence you exude lend credibility to your message.

Most of the time, you will be interviewed in a sitting position. Sitting upright, slightly leaning forward towards the interviewer, keeping your gestures close to your upper body are all standard techniques that work well on-screen.

No matter what you say, you have to look (and feel) convinced if you want to be credible. A classic example of the importance of being "telegenic" is the Nixon-Kennedy presidential debate of September 26, 1960. Nixon had been sick and looked pale, but when he saw that Kennedy (who was tanned from outdoor sport activities) didn't put on makeup, he refused it as well. It was an evenly matched debate, but on screen, Nixon looked uncomfortable, his shirt didn't fit well, and he was disconcerted by Kennedy's confidence and charisma.

For those who listened to the "Great Debate" on the radio, Nixon was the winner. However, Kennedy was the clear winner for those watching the debate on TV. Needless to say, this had quite an effect on the voters and the election of 1960.

Practice

All these recommendations are not a substitute for practicing extensively before the interview. Practice your lines several times before the actual interview; this will help make sure your word choice is accurate and your style natural. Nothing will get you better prepared than a session with a good media trainer, and even then, things don't always go as planned. So, practice, practice, practice. If you can't afford a media trainer, ask a colleague or a friend to simulate the interview with you so you can get a full rehearsal. Even better, have someone video tape you so you can look at yourself while listening to yourself speak.

Common Mistakes when being Interviewed

Speaking Too Fast

Fast-paced information is one thing, but talking too fast is quite another. The faster you speak, the less understandable you will be—especially if English is not your native language. Get to the point, avoid repetitions, stay on message—all the while speaking at a normal pace. Often we find ourselves speaking too fast when we are either nervous or upset—and we let ourselves get carried away.

Talking About Too Many Things

Don't try to cram all your thoughts into one interview. Be selective. Mention only what is useful and relevant for your core message (remember, you prepared that). If you bring up too many details, none will stick with the audience. In addition, it will make you speak too fast, which, in turn, will make you less understandable (see above).

Being All Business

Failing to establish a personal rapport with the reporters can be detrimental. Be nice and friendly, find common ground, and establish a rapport. It will help put you at greater ease and be more effective. Try to always keep your cool when dealing with a journalist—understand that some nervousness and perhaps even a hurt ego are part of the game. Whatever your feelings about a given question or the reporter's attitude during the interview, don't show them: don't argue or become defensive. A combative answer makes for great TV or for a good print quote—that is, good for the reporter, not for you.

Forgetting or Ignoring a Deadline

Timing is everything in the media business. If you want to be treated seriously by the media, you need to deliver what they want, when they want it. Once you promise to be available at a certain time or to send a given piece of information by a certain day, do so! Otherwise, you'll burn your bridges very quickly.

Restating a Negative Comment

Sometimes we are tempted to deny an accusation or a wrong statement directly, but by repeating negative words, we actually amplify their echo effect. For example:

Reporter: "According to the xyz report, your revenues went down twenty percent last year. How do you respond to that?"

Typical answer: "Actually, our revenues did not go down twenty percent last year. They increased by five percent."

A better answer: "Our revenues actually went up by five percent last year." Notice how this answer just emphasizes the positive (the revenue uptick) rather than repeating a negative (the revenue downturn).

Rephrasing a Loaded Question

Again, don't repeat a misleading comment. If the reporter says, "There is widespread speculation that your business unit will be up for sale unless it reaches the new revenue targets," you might feel on the defensive and respond as follows: "If you are asking me whether my company will sell this business unit if it doesn't reach its revenue targets, I can't comment on that."

Instead, rephrase the sentence in a positive way: "The issue here is reaching the business unit's revenue targets. I believe we are well positioned to do so."

Never let your guard down, especially if you are talking about a controversial topic.

Speculating

If you don't know, simply say so and refer the question to the most appropriate person.

Embellishing the Truth

Don't lie. Lies find their way to the front page, eventually. Always tell the truth, however difficult it seems, and you'll avoid further damage.

Filling in the Silence

An interview is not a casual conversation. Don't feel obligated to keep the dialogue going, as it is the reporter's responsibility to do so, not yours. Beware of those reporters who try to get you to talk and talk, as you run the risk of divulging too much information.

The "Media" Risk

A few years ago, a group of students attending a prestigious U.S. business school were interviewed just outside their campus. The reporter was very friendly and seemed genuinely interested. So the students engaged in a candid and freewheeling conversation with the reporter. Little did they know that their remarks would end up soon afterward on a major business weekly publication. Or that the dean would have to deal with the fallout of that interview as, later that year, the business school plummeted in major national rankings.

Always keep in mind that even a spontaneous, informal exchange with a reporter can end up poorly if you don't know the rules of the game.

USEFUL TIPS FOR DEALING WITH THE U.S. MEDIA

Helpful

Knowing your goals

Having an interesting story and a clear message

Backing up your points with facts and figures

Distilling your message into sound bites

Practicing your lines

Doing you research

Looking good

Harmful

Being vague and long-winded

Not looking the part

Not researching the reporter/publication ahead of time

Overreacting and taking questions personally

Speaking too fast

Speculating

9 Speaking English Like a Leader

Many of our foreign-born clients come to us for help in learning how to sound like a leader in English. Typically, their English is already very good, their vocabulary pretty extensive, and while they may have an accent, they normally make few grammatical mistakes, if any. What exactly do they mean then, when they say they want to speak like a leader? In our experience, what they want to do is speak in a manner that makes them appear competent and persuasive—they want to sound smart, confident, and powerful.

Unfortunately, the concept of leadership and how it expresses itself in language is a very difficult one to define. There are many books with various leadership theories—and we certainly don't want to add another one to the already long list.

But we do know that foreign-born professionals face a particularly difficult challenge: not only is leadership (and its components) hard to define, its characteristics are also culturally bound.

The language patterns of leadership are different from language to language. The language patterns of Chinese or German leaders can be the opposite of those typical of an American leader. A business leader in Germany uses a very erudite, complex, rich language full of subordinate clauses and adjectives, so the tendency for a native speaker of German is to replicate that pattern in English. However, that's precisely what makes him/her sound like a foreigner in the U.S. Similarly, a Chinese business leader sprinkles his or her sentences with a number of high-sounding slogans and maxims (e.g., "restructuring leads to progress"), but that approach doesn't work here.

Many foreigners (unless they are already bilingual) have a tendency to translate from their native language and use some of the same linguistic patterns—especially if they are under stress. That's part of the problem. If you want to come across as a leader in your professional field in the U.S., you have to borrow from the same repertoire of techniques that American leaders use: brief, concise statements, simple language, and clear messages.

What really matters is clarity of thought, expressed in simple, good English. If you want to speak English with authority, you need to steer clear of the erudite eloquence and rhetorical techniques that are typical of leadership in other cultures, and focus on presenting an effective message instead.

Often foreign-born professionals worry about using incorrect words, or picking inappropriate expressions, or repeating overused adjectives. They worry that these language choices make them sound uneducated and more junior than they actually are. While we understand this preoccupation with individual words, we have found that what contributes to form an impression of authority, or detracts from it, has to do with having a clear message and a straightforward sentence structure. The individual words you use don't matter as much; even if you pick a very unusual word, it might be noticed, but it will usually be understood in the context.

Two Approaches

Franz Josef, an Austrian project manager at a high-tech company in Silicon Valley, was asked by his boss during a team meeting whether he thought that a coworker, Ann (who was really keen on taking on a leadership role in the project), would be able to run the project. He replied in a convoluted way: "If you are an avid runner and are training for a 10K race and you finish among the first 50 runners, that doesn't mean you would qualify for the Olympics." His team members were perplexed and didn't know what he was talking about.

What would an American have said?

Allison, sitting in the same team meeting, replied: "I think that Ann is a really great person, I like her a lot, although I don't know her well. I'm a bit concerned about her lack of direct experience. But I suppose we could give it a try. And, we are always here to help her out in case she needs us."

Both project managers were expressing the same idea: they had some hesitations about Ann. However, Franz Josef's example was confusing and vague, and sounded negative. Allison's approach was straightforward and positive. Their choice of language and their attitudes were fundamentally different and influenced their team members' perception of their abilities as leaders.

This chapter tries to give a few pointers on how leadership in the U.S. can be expressed and perceived through the use of the English language. The goal is to make our readers more aware of the subtext and the subtleties of their linguistic choices (especially the subconscious ones) and to help them learn to use English more deliberately. We all know that people skills are important for career advancement, and language plays a big role in interacting well with your colleagues, superiors, and subordinates alike.

We realize that some of the points discussed below may come across as generalizations or even as gross simplifications. They are all based on real-life examples of issues faced by our clients or other foreign-born professionals with whom we have worked. The techniques discussed are only meant to be general principles and should be considered illustrations of some of the language patterns typical of accomplished professionals in the U.S. (especially Silicon Valley). Consider them as a menu of options from which you can choose to craft your own style of speaking English as a leader.

Convergence toward the Middle of the Language Spectrum

Think about language as a continuum of possible choices, with one end being explicit, direct, forceful language and the other end being indirect, hesitant language. Europeans (and Israelis even more so) can be seen at the end of the explicit side of the spectrum, sometimes using overheated language, while many Asian cultures tend to be at the other end of the "indirect language" side.

Americans, on the other hand, tend to be more in the middle of this spectrum, with a tendency towards direct but calm and diplomatic language. An American would say: "I am not sure he is fully qualified," whereas a European would say: "I don't think he is qualified," and an Asian might say: "I am not really familiar with his qualifications."

In business, Americans generally express themselves in measured tones. You will rarely hear words expressed in rage or even in overblown enthusiasm in meetings, on the phone, and in conferences. Employees are expected to be in control of their emotions and to be constructive members of the team, with a positive attitude, to "not make waves" or to not stand out in a conspicuous way. For example, in a recent discussion at a big, high-tech Silicon Valley company, a professional visiting from overseas started angrily attacking a colleague who worked overseas. Immediately, one of the senior managers stepped in and told him that in the U.S., personal attacks were not allowed and asked him to please stick to issues and problems.

Even during an argument, raised voices are not acceptable; the discussion should retain a certain level of politeness and should never get personal—personal attacks are considered the height of being "unprofessional." It is OK to disagree about issues, but not about someone's personal input. So while a question such as "How can you say something like this?" might work in some parts of Europe, it is not advisable to use this kind of tone here.

At the opposite end, being too indirect is also a handicap. Some of our Asian clients agonize over meetings in which they have to "confront" an employee with negative news. The implicit conflict is not manageable for them, and it forces them to express themselves very indirectly, which frustrates Americans because they can't really understand what the problem is. So, many of them choose to avoid the dreaded confrontation altogether.

In the business world in the U.S., there is a certain uniformity of language, i.e., a tendency to conform to certain models of communication and behavior within an office or industry. Corporate America, in general, is more accepting of people who fit in—even in terms of language—than of people who behave in an eccentric fashion. However, this tendency to conform—also called "drinking the same Kool-Aid"[19]—is less common in start-ups, where "being different" is encouraged and people tend to conform less to prescribed behaviors.

A Menu of Techniques to Speak Like a Leader

Be Positive

Use language that emphasizes the positive rather than the negative. For example, a sentence like, "We cannot offer you a job right now although we do anticipate several openings in September," sounds much better if it's revised with a positive spin: "We might have an opening for you in September, although not right now. We'll get in touch with you then."

Using sentences that emphasize solutions rather than problems is what distinguishes a style that is perceived as a leadership style. A solutions-based approach makes your statements sound positive and geared towards solving the problem—and being able to shift emphasis from the problem to the solution really shapes people's perception of you as a leader.

Another example: "The new equipment will not be subject to as many breakdowns as the old voice mail system, thereby eliminating lost time." Positive spin: "The new voice mail system will save time by eliminating the many breakdowns we had with the old system."

---

19. "Drinking your own Kool-Aid" is a typical Silicon Valley expression.

Stay positive even when it feels impossible, e.g., when you are assigned a project that is really a stretch and seems unachievable. Don't say: "I can't guarantee I will be able to finish the job by Wednesday, but I'll try my best," but rather say: "I will do everything I can to get the job done by Wednesday."

Frequently, foreigners will react with skepticism or even sarcasm when they hear a very positive, almost glowing statement or speech: it sounds too good to be true to them. They think the speaker is being too naïve and disingenuous. We remember a European client of ours who had a very cynical reaction to the "good news" speech delivered by a senior executive in her company. Her American colleagues were put off by her sarcastic remarks, and she didn't earn any points—as she might have in Europe—with her questioning attitude.

Get to the Point Quickly

English is all about economy of words.

When you want to make a statement, especially in a meeting or conference call, get to the point quickly. Emphasize the bottom line [your main point], and specify what you want people to do as a result of your comment. Vague explanations and long sentences will label you as ineffective.

For example, "Changing consumer demographics and psychographics will enable mainstream information technology if vendors get it right."

Revised: "Consumer trends will make information technology mainstream. Vendors need to 'get it right' immediately."

A good technique, especially when the thought you are trying to express is fairly complex, is to use enumeration techniques and/or "chunking down" problems.

For example: "What I think needs to happen is 1, 2, 3..." or: "Let's look at this problem from a couple of perspectives: perspective A..., perspective B..."

Being verbose and long-winded is a sure way to lose your audience quickly. Get to the point you want to make and keep it simple.

Use Active Instead of Passive Sentences

Active sentences give an impression of empowerment. Already in middle school, Americans students are taught to use the active versus the passive tense. The active form sounds much more compelling. Listen to the difference.

Passive: "Hourly workers were found to take as much pride as salaried workers in their company affiliations."

Active: "The research team found that hourly workers take as much pride as salaried workers in their company affiliation."

Use Verbs Instead of Nouns

In many languages other than English, people use more nouns than verbs when speaking in an educated manner. However, American English focuses on using more verbs than nouns. Instead of saying, "The expectation of management is that the recovery of the economy is imminent," you should try, "Management expects the economy to recover soon." Not only does this sound better, it is also a much easier way to communicate for non-native English speakers once they have learned to think this way.

Use Questions Rather than Statements

One of the main problems for international professionals—as we mentioned before—is that they tend to translate from their native language, especially when stressed or overworked, and so while their sentences might be grammatically correct, they don't strike the same note in English.

A good technique is to turn assertions into questions. Instead of saying: "Send me the contract" which would sound like a command in English, try a softer sentence: "Can you please send me the contract?" or even better: "When do you think you will be able to send me the contract?"

"Call me tomorrow" is a direct request (almost an order) that sounds quite rude in a business environment. Better: "Can you call me tomorrow?"

But not all questions are OK. Direct questions can sound aggressive and controlling. For example, instead of asking: "Have you received approval from management to do this?" a better version is: "I was wondering if you have received approval yet."

And, if you would like to know if someone is "on board", it is best to ask, "Let me ask you this, are you sure you can commit to this now?" rather than: "Will you follow through?"

Don't Be Too Modest

Sometimes foreigners—especially women from a more indirect, less individualistic culture—will use phrases that undercut their authority, making them sound weak and ineffective. They will say, "I don't know if this makes any sense to you" or, "I'm sure you already thought about this" or, "I am sure Mr. Smith knows more about this than I do, but..."

Or, they will apologize all the time: "Forgive me for interrupting..."

Avoid these disclaimers as much as you can. Far from enhancing your authority, they detract from it.

Be Diplomatic

In order to fit in, to be heard in a positive way, you frequently need to strike a diplomatic tone.

"We've already done that in the past," sounds rude in English. A native speaker would most likely say: "It seems to me we have tried this approach before."

Instead of making definite assertions and talking in black and white terms, it is advisable to use many phrases like "I think..., my impression is..."

When someone stops talking, instead of immediately providing your own input, it is better to use a phrase such as, "If I heard you correctly, this is what you were suggesting..." or "Let me make sure I understand you correctly."

Other commonly used phrases are: "Did I hear you say that you were going to do X and Y…?

"Help me understand what you mean by saying…"

These sentences help make sure that the speaker feels acknowledged, and they allow you to formulate a more careful reply.

Be Polite

As discussed, U.S. English makes a great effort to soften any blow. Just adding some polite words such as "please" or "do me a favor," doesn't do the trick here. "Please don't make that mistake again" is not an acceptable way of addressing a coworker. A better version could be: "Could this procedure be looked at differently next time?" It avoids an accusatory tone and asks a question, which is much easier to accept than a statement, as it leaves room for discussion. And, it focuses on the issue instead of the person.

There are many other ways of softening your language and still getting the idea across. For example, instead of saying: "Can you wait for me to finish this?" you might want to use the conditional tense and say: "Would you please have a seat and wait for a moment?" (See how soft this suggestion was?)

Another technique is to add a "maybe" to requests or statements, such as: "Maybe we could look at this again when we have more data," or "Maybe I didn't look at this from all angles, I'll go back and do it again." The expression "quite" also softens the blow, as in: "That wasn't quite what I was expecting." Another option to defuse difficult situations is: "It seems to me that…" or "I think this could be rethought…"

And, if you don't know something, don't just shrug and blame someone else: "I don't have a clue about this. Herr Mueller was supposed to prepare it." Rather, say that you will look it up, discuss it with Herr Mueller, and get back to them.

Conversely, foreigners themselves might also encounter situations and questions from their U.S. counterparts that seem rude to them, depending on what culture they come from. For example, even after much explanation, they might be asked: "What do you mean, what's the bottom line?" or "What does this have to do with anything?"

When faced with what they perceive as rude questions, or even verbal attacks, many foreigners are taken aback and say whatever comes to their mind; they are not prepared to answer or, if they do, their discomfort with the question might easily come through with an aggressive comment. The best strategy is to rephrase the question and say, "What do you mean?" or, "Are you asking me if..." or even better, "Why do you ask?"

Use Familiar Examples

Avoid unfamiliar examples because it takes time to explain them. For example, many of our French clients interweave French historical figures in their speech; that's not a wise thing to do because many people here aren't familiar with European history (and they don't have to be).

Use the Right Intonation

Understand that when you raise your voice at the end of a sentence, people hear it as a question and not as a statement. Sometimes called "uptalk," this is a habit many foreign-born professional women display, and their credibility takes a hit [is undermined]. One of our clients would introduce herself as: "I am a product manager," but she raised her voice at the end of the sentence. It sounded as if she were not sure of her position.

Listen Actively

This is another characteristic of the language of leadership in the U.S. Business leaders in the U.S. are required to manage by consensus and therefore need to make sure that they have heard what you are saying and will try to capture your contribution. Please see Chapter 7 for a description of active listening techniques.

A nice way to end a discussion is to summarize what was said without putting in your own interpretation. Not only does that show that you were paying attention, but also that you were able to put it into context without judgment, thereby validating the other person's position.

Also, active listening can help you contribute your point of view in a meeting without your having to wait until you are called upon; use transitions like "What I am hearing is…" and then state your own point.

Adapt Your Language to Different Hierarchical Situations

It's undeniable that language changes depending on your position of power. Therefore, a shift in language patterns is necessary depending on whether you are talking to your boss or subordinate. This can present serious challenges to foreign-born professionals when they are promoted to positions of leadership. Should they now adopt a more forceful language, which is how, in many of their cultures, a leader is believed to communicate? Or should they remain one of the guys with the group out of which they rose to the new managerial position? There is no bulletproof solution, as every situation is different. In general, however, people's tones tend to move from more deferential (subordinate to boss) to more definitive.

Let's look at a few examples of how the same issue—a delay in getting to a meeting—would be expressed in different ways depending on the hierarchical relationship:

- Subordinate to boss: "We had to get the meeting started… we weren't sure if you were going to make it." A more hesitant, subdued tone.

- Peer to peer: "Helen, how come you're late? Did something happen?" A friendly reproach.

- Boss to subordinate: "Prashant, you came in late again today and you didn't warn us ahead of time. In the future, please call and let us know and I will regard this as an isolated incidence." Very matter-of-fact, straightforward, still respectful in tone.

How Do You Give and Receive Feedback in the U.S. Business Culture?

Business leaders are often responsible for giving feedback. For foreign-born professionals, it is very important to know and understand the formula used here when giving feedback in the U.S. Positive feedback is rather straightforward and it will be punctuated by adjectives like "great" or, "good job" or, "way to go."

Negative feedback will almost always start with a positive statement or several positive general statements, so that the atmosphere is more relaxed and one is not just focusing on things that need improving. Once the positive points have been made, the next word is usually a BUT; this is the turning point, and people realize that what comes next is really what the review is all about. However, because positive comments are also part of the equation, the feedback is more acceptable and is not perceived as criticism. For more on this topic, see Chapter 2.

SPEAKING TIPS TO IMPROVE YOUR LANGUAGE SKILLS

1. Keep your sentences short
2. Prefer the simple to the complex
3. Prefer the familiar word
4. Avoid unnecessary words
5. Put action into your verbs
6. Get to the point quickly
7. Have one clear message
8. Be positive
9. Use terms your listener can picture
10. Talk to express your point, not to impress your audience

Reducing Your Accent

A young European private equity analyst was enjoying a very success-
ful professional life in the U.S. Even though he realized he was seen
as a somewhat eccentric, brilliant outsider, it didn't bother him until he
started noticing some perplexed reactions when he talked during his
firm's partners' meetings. He was frequently asked to repeat what he
just said, and still people looked at him perplexed. One day, a senior
partner at his firm pulled him aside and explained to him that what he
said and the way he said it attracted attention simply because of his
accent. His accent and intonation forced his colleagues to really con-
centrate on his words and, therefore, made most exchanges fairly la-
borious. Together, they concluded that his accent was holding him
back from fitting in more smoothly.

The more you advance in your career, the more your accent matters.
Having an accent is not a problem "per se," since Silicon Valley and the
Bay Area are full of international professionals. But if your accent inter-
feres with your being understood, or if it is so noticeable that it is dis-
tracting, then it does matter. And it can get in the way of your
professional development.

The good news is that, despite conventional wisdom, you can modify
your accent even as an adult. Below is a process that has helped
dozens of our clients. One important point to understand is that while
you will be able to modify your accent, you will probably never lose it—
nor should you. The "flatter" the world becomes, as Thomas Friedman
points out,[20] the more accents are a normal occurrence.

Steps to Gradually Reduce Your Accent

Set goals. Know what you can realistically expect to change during and
after the sessions; this also depends on the amount of work you put
into hearing and improving different sounds and word emphases.

Practice. Every day, even on the weekend, practice the new sounds
and words. Stand in front of the mirror, watch the way your mouth
makes the sound, and really focus on how you are enunciating the

---

20. Friedman, Thomas. <u>The World is Flat</u>. New York: Farrar, Straus and
Giroux, 2005.

sound you need to improve. You will need to train the muscles to behave in new ways. So be sure to relax your jaw and the back of your throat.

Watch yourself in the mirror to see if your mouth and tongue are in the correct positions. For example, if you don't see your tongue placed visibly between your teeth to make the /th/ sound, you probably aren't doing it correctly. Develop the consciousness of listening to yourself—in your mind—and of anticipating what you are going to say. Here is a typical process of correcting your accented words:

1st phase: Here comes the word. Darn, I said it incorrectly.

2nd phase: Oops, I said it incorrectly again, but at least now I know how it should sound, and I knew it was coming.

3rd phase: Here comes the word. I know how to say it. Success!

Pay particular attention to the consonants in the middle and at the end of the words: without them, you will be hard to understand. /Have/ is not the same as /ha/, or /five/ can't be pronounced /fi/. This is difficult for most Asians as such sounds don't exist in Asian languages. For example, during a recent accent reduction session, a Chinese engineer said something that sounded like: /I ha essampl fi paymen contra/. What he meant was: "I have an example of five payment contracts."

Pay attention to vowel sounds (a, e, i, o, u, y) and diphthongs (ei, ai, ou, au, oa, oi); some of them are held longer than others. For more tips and ideas, please go to
http://www.professional-business-communications.com.

Slow down! Post a sticky note with these words next to your telephone and write them ("slow down") into your presentation notes. This will remind you to slow down when you catch yourself talking too fast during your presentation or phone call—especially if you are stressed.

American English goes up in sound and then comes down, so listen to yourself: are you constantly using a high/upward tone at the end of your sentences? This will confuse your listeners because they will think you are asking a question and not making a point. Lower your voice at the end of a sentence or thought.

Record yourself and listen to your own speech.

Check if you sound boring, as monotonous speech is hard to listen to.

Videotape yourself and critique yourself (or have a friend do it).

Read. Read, read, read in English as much as you have time for; read a minimum of half an hour every day. Your reading should include fiction, with dialogue in it so that everyday words in American English become totally natural to you, as well as sentence structure.

Read along with books on tape, record yourself and compare the sounds.

Watch TV. Watch programs such as the news, PBS, sitcoms [situation comedies], etc. Listen to the way people sound out the words and listen to the music of their sentences.

Talk to people outside of your language group as much as you can.

Take at least 5 to 10 minutes every day to practice the new sounds; the best place is on the phone because no one can watch you if you don't look graceful at the beginning.

Correct your "sloppy" speech. If you already have been speaking English for a long time, it is possible that you have developed bad habits and are 'sloppy' saying certain words. Watch out for them and correct them; sound them out for a while in a really exaggerated manner; then, when you say them in a conversation, they will sound correct.

Techniques to Increase Your Vocabulary

Reading Books

Many of our clients are engineers who typically read nonfiction books, if any. Reading fiction will help you learn new words and expressions. Choose one from the *New York Times* Bestseller List, or on any topic of interest to you (historical fiction, detective novels, mysteries). Be sure to choose books with a lot of dialogue, as this will help make your own conversations more fluent.

Listening to Audio Books

If you don't have much time to read, you can listen to audio books while driving to and from work. Borrow CDs from your local library or download audio books directly to your iPod from sites such as http://www.audible.com.

Watching News, Nature, Technical or Political Shows on TV, or Listening to NPR

The TV and radio can be your good friends if you choose shows that interest you. Listen actively to the words and expressions that people use and write down any that are new to you.

Joining Toastmasters

Toastmasters is an organization that helps people learn how to speak well in any situations. If you want to be exposed to a variety of topics and vocabulary, you can join your local chapter of Toastmasters. Many of the big companies in Silicon Valley, such as HP or Sun Microsystems, have internal Toastmaster groups. You will have a chance to practice any new words you have learned.

Going to Business Events

There are so many opportunities to go to events on current business or political issues. Possible sources are: a university or college, your local chamber of commerce, meetup.com, Craigslist, alumni groups, and U.S. and international business organizations (in Silicon Valley alone

there are over two hundred organizations listed at
http://www.svhub. org). Groups such as AAMA, BAIA, CSPA, GABA, Hispanic Net, HYSTA, Monte Jade, SDForum, SiliconFrench, SIPA, SVASE, TiE and so on are very active in Silicon Valley. There are similar groups all over the U.S.; it is just a matter of finding them.

Making Flash Cards of New and Idiomatic Expressions

Listen attentively to your American friends and colleagues, and write down the expressions they use frequently that you are not familiar with. Make sure you know what they mean before you make them a part of your own vocabulary.

In order to keep the words memorized, make yourself flash cards and go through them every day in the beginning; as you get better at them, you can study the cards once a week and keep them active.

One of our clients would write down all the words that the VPs used in meetings, and tried to incorporate them into his vocabulary. It's a good exercise for everybody: make a list of words used by people you respect, and see which ones you can start using.

Joining a Book Club

If you have the time, join a book club. This will "force" you to read since the club members will expect you to participate in the discussions.

Studying SAT Vocabulary Books

If you want to learn more words quickly, buy a book with SAT vocabulary. SAT stands for Standard Achievement Test and is the test that most high school seniors are expected to take to get into college. These books usually have about 250 of the most commonly used words educated people apply in conversation and in their written expressions.

Here are a few phrases that always work well when talking to your boss:[21]

LIST OF POWERFUL PHRASES IN ENGLISH

achieve goals

adjust our priorities

best use of resources

best for the company, for the team

big picture

cost in resources

cost in time

give full credit to

give this a trial

I need your advice

increased market, productivity

opens up possibilities

run all the numbers

take the upside

team player

thank you for asking me

think this through

user friendly

win-win situation

you have a good point

---

21. This list was excerpted from Griffin, Jack. How to Say it at Work: Putting Yourself Across with Power Words, Phrases, Body Language and Communication Secrets. New York: Prentice Hall Press, 1998.

CORPORATE JARGON

Ramping it up—to increase

Let's talk offline—let's have a private conversation

Pinging—sending a quick greeting (usually via e-mail)

Key differentiator—key difference, main difference

Sharing best practices—compare best ideas

Scrubbing or window-dressing the numbers—manipulating the numbers

Going granular—talking, discussing in great detail

Come off the reservation—relate to real life*

Leverage your positioning—to exert power or influence on

Spinning—couching the message in a way that is appealing to the listeners, highlighting or rephrasing certain aspects of the message to get your point across

Micromanaging—managing with excessive attention to details

We are on the same page—we agree

They siloed—different business units become silos, entities by themselves, thereby assuming too much power

Violently agreeing to something—agreeing

Coming to a hard stop—you can only do something until that stop [time]

Taking the ball and running with it—being responsible for a certain project

* This expression does not have a negative connotation in the business world.

Action Steps to Sound More Confident

1. Use precise vocabulary that shows your expertise, not complicated words and convoluted phrases.

2. Describe what you mean clearly, and don't leave room for ambiguity.

3. Adapt your vocabulary to the position and background of the person with whom you are speaking; establish a connection.

4. Involve your colleagues in your speech; use conversational tags at the end of sentences, e.g., "You would see it the same way, wouldn't you?" or "I understand you have expertise in this field, don't you?"

5. Use simple, straightforward sentences

6. Don't use words and expressions that convey superiority or inferiority such as, "Am I the only one who...?"

7. Be positive; turn sentences with negatives into sentences with a positive spin.

8. Don't use sarcasm or irony in formal or informal speeches, as these can be misinterpreted.

9. Use words that encourage others to open up and contribute, and you will be seen as a powerful listener and communicator.

USEFUL TIPS FOR SPEAKING ENGLISH LIKE A LEADER

Helpful
Having a clear message
Understanding and using idioms correctly
Using positive language and expressions
Speaking in verbs, rather than in nouns
Being polite
Slowing down
Reading books in fiction and nonfiction to improve your vocabulary and fluency

Harmful
Using unusual words
Being cynical and sarcastic
Swearing and using vulgar language
Not listening
Mistaking informality for lack of hierarchy
Speaking with a strong accent

10 Why and How to Network

Hamburg, Germany: Dr. Schiller, the CEO of a small company that specializes in Web site optimization, is going to an event where he thinks he can meet new clients. The dress code is formal; suit and tie for men, dresses with jackets or suits for women. As he enters the room, everyone is standing and looking around quite uncomfortable, each with a drink in hand. All of a sudden, the CEO sees a young man walking around with a sign that says: Dr. Schmidt is looking for Dr. Schiller. There is movement in the crowd as the two men meet each other. They talk for about half an hour.

Then the CEO joins a group of people and introduces himself as Dr. Schiller; he explains what his company does in great detail and lectures the small crowd about the benefits of adopting his product very matter-of-factly. Everybody takes a few minutes to give a rather detailed overview of their company. Then they exchange cards and leave the event, glad they have made a useful contact. Within a week, everybody follows up with a package of company literature to their new contacts.

Jump to a networking event on the West Coast. The CEO of a small start-up is informally dressed, has packed 50 business cards, and did some online research on the people he is likely to meet at the event he is attending. When he gets there, he grabs a drink and starts seeking out people (identified by their name tags and company affiliation) to whom he can introduce himself. After chatting with them for a few minutes, he excuses himself to go to the buffet, gets some food and moves on to another group of attendees. He spends the next hour talking to as many people as he can, and after he leaves the event he takes a moment in his car to write any important details on the business cards he collected, so he will remember the people he talked to.

Why are these two networking events handled so differently? Because people in the U.S. are, in general, comfortable networking: they learn the importance of networking early on and practice it starting in college.

What is Networking and Why is it Important?

Networking is a way of life here. For most people in the U.S., networking is just part of how they grew up, and they develop the necessary skills very gradually and naturally.

Networking is about making deliberate connections and cultivating them to further your own goals as well as the goals of others. What separates networking from pure socializing is that networking has clear objectives, requires a focused approach, and generates action items and follow-up activities from every encounter.

Good networking is a two-way street—you can network effectively only if you are also thinking: "What can I do for this person?"

Networking is also a good way to make friends and acquaintances. If you are new to a city, the networking groups you join can help you find your way around and may also become the source for new friends, as you do have a common connection.

In addition, networking is a crucial part of looking for a job. But you shouldn't start networking when you are unemployed, because it takes time to build a good network of contacts and you don't want to be perceived as desperately needy (you do need a job—now). By net-working actively during the times when you are fully employed, you will already have contacts who may lead you to your next job when you decide to move on.

Since networking boils down to the ability to have informal business conversations with anybody, anywhere, it is even more crucial if you are self-employed. You can take the opportunity to promote your business, your interests, your passions, whenever you go to the gym, when you have drink in a coffee shop, or stand in line at the movie.

However, networking doesn't come naturally to most foreigners. Espe-cially if you come from a culture where socializing is more happen-stance than a choice, you are most likely going to be uncomfortable networking.

In fact, in our business practice we have noticed that one of the main problems for foreign-born professionals is how to network effectively at social events, especially for those from Asian cultures—Chinese as well as Indian professionals in Silicon Valley. For example, all the events they attend at various professional organizations during the holiday season, Thanksgiving, or the Fourth of July weekend could (and should) turn into networking opportunities for them. But despite all the invitations they receive, it is not easy for them to make good contacts. So they tend to stick with their compatriots or with their stable group of acquaintances. And yet, networking would be a crucial skill for them to master precisely because they want to (or need to) expand their contacts base.

All international professionals should actively try to make networking part of their life. This chapter tries to lay out a road map on how to network effectively for those who need to sharpen their social skills.

Where to Network

There are many opportunities for networking. Possible starting points are your local Chamber of Commerce, a local Rotary or Lions Club, a local university or college, or the local alumni group of your Alma Mater. Also, take a look at local chapters of professional organizations (in Silicon Valley alone there are over two hundred organizations listed at http://www.svhub.org). Groups such as AAMA, BAIA, CSPA, GABA, Hispanic Net, HYSTA, Monte Jade, SDForum, SiliconFrench, SIPA, SVASE, TiE and so on are very active in the Bay Area. There are similar groups all over the U.S.; it is just a matter of finding them.

You could also check out meetup.com, Craigslist, interesting blogs with a local angle, and city Web sites; you can check Google for business interest groups in your area (both U.S. and internationally focused); and finally, simply ask people around you.

Once you have found a few groups that interest you, go to several meetings and see if you feel comfortable and if people are friendly to newcomers. When you have decided on the three or four groups whose meetings you want to attend, it is really important to start attending them on a regular basis. That way you will get to know people, as it takes quite a while to build meaningful relationships. A good way to connect faster is offering to volunteer to help with the events. You'll get to see the members more often, and they will learn to appreciate you more quickly.

Don't always stay in your "comfort zone," but rather try to deliberately seek out people and groups who have interests you might want to learn about; as a result, you will grow those networking "branches" which will allow you to branch out from your initial contact base.

A Stanford business school professor a few years ago gave a talk about how to grow a network. He pointed out that it is better to attend a variety of groups that are thematically unrelated. This way you will not always meet the same people, and you will widen the scope of your networking considerably.

How to Network Effectively (and Have Fun, Too)

How do you engage in a meaningful conversation about business in a social setting? How do you smoothly turn a casual chat into a productive exchange? Are there different rules of the game depending on whom you are speaking to? Are there any rules at all that are distinctive to U.S. culture alone?

If networking is not second nature for you [doesn't come easily to you], you might want to follow the approach described below. It is a simple plan that has helped many of our international clients navigate an area which seems so treacherous to them.

1. The first rule is: don't panic! Preparation is the best way to go to networking events and to emerge "victorious," having not only survived but also having met some interesting people to reconnect with again at future events.

2. Make a plan ahead of time, especially if you are shy or not used to networking. For example, decide that you will stay a minimum of forty-five minutes, talk to at least four people, and get their business cards—then you can leave. That makes it easier for you to go to the event, as you have given yourself permission to leave after a (predetermined) amount of time, and you will still have accomplished something.

3. Take someone along to the event. You can't use that person as a shield, so you will still have to meet new people—but having a friend to come back to is always helpful.

4. Do some research before the event. Find out who will attend and what kind of interests the group has. Prepare topics of conversation ahead of time: current sports events, volunteer groups you belong to, children, schools they attend or you attended, hobbies, travels. The easiest way to get the conversation going is to ask for (genuine) advice from someone who seems to be knowledgeable about your interests: where to play the best golf in the area, how to start playing tennis, what new books are worth reading, where to get ethnic foods, and so on.

5. Prepare to introduce yourself to groups already standing together and talking. This is the hard part: go up to the group, then pleasantly make eye contact, and usually someone will ask for your name or will introduce him- or herself. You can quickly give your name and pick up the conversation where it had left off, and you will fit right in.

6. Go up to someone standing alone. Often there are people at events who feel as intimidated as you might be feeling. Go up to anyone standing alone, talk to the person for a while, and if you

don't know how to end the conversation when you want to move on, suggest that you both join a group that is somewhere else in the room.

7. Don't dominate the conversation. Keep the conversation light. Most Americans don't like to talk about illness, death, or politics. Perhaps you can make a nice comment on the event, the panel topic, the food, or maybe you can discover an acquaintance you have in common—which is quite frequent in the Silicon Valley as most people work in the IT industry.

8. Watch your body language. No one wants to talk to someone who is hunched over looking at the floor or looking like "a deer in the headlights" [frozen expression of someone surprised and caught unaware]. Try your best to exude confidence by standing straight with a smile on your face (or something like a smile), and look people in the eye.

9. Don't drink too much alcohol, or better yet, just stick to water. We have seen too many people become too "relaxed" because of too many alcoholic drinks, which obviously didn't help their networking goals. If you don't like water, choose a carbonated beverage.

10. If you get many business cards, write some kind of description of the person you met on the back. If during the evening you get a lot of business cards and start worrying that you will forget who was who, go to a quiet corner and quickly write something on the back that will jog your memory the next day. Be sure to follow up on anything you promised to do or send.

Have fun and remember that you don't have to stay the whole evening. But also remember that in order to really network effectively, you need to make a commitment to yourself to attend events regularly and contribute to them actively with insightful conversation.

Tips for Effective Conversations

Elevator Pitch

Before going to events, you need to have practiced a short, effective speech describing yourself and your business or profession. People are not known here for their patience, so you need to get it right the first time. Keep it simple, short, and intriguing.

Prepare Points for Conversation

Research the organizations, look at their Web sites, read up on what their last events were, check for any news coverage. To get a feeling of the profile of members, "Google" their names or check them out on LinkedIn. This will give you an idea of what the topics of conversation might be. Even if you are going to an event that is not directly business-related, yet you expect that some business topics might come up, see what kind of background or education the other participants have. This will give you a leg up [an advantage] in bringing up topics that you know will be of interest.

Another good idea is to find out about people's families from their own conversations, or keep track of their hobbies, and follow up on that each time you see them.

What matters is that you are genuinely interested and that you are also prepared to share some personal information.

Exercise

1. Practice your elevator pitch.
   Take three minutes, craft a twenty-word sentence that summarizes who you are/what you do. Rehearse in front of a mirror.
2. Make a list of conversation starters.
   Select three topics: one from your professional world, one from the daily news, and one based on developments in the organization whose event you are attending.

Choose Your Topics Well

First of all, keep the conversation light. The classic topics that are taboo in light conversation are sex, religion, money, and politics. Most Americans also don't like to talk about illness, death, or other sad topics.

Never say anything negative, especially if you don't know the other participants well enough. Criticism and complaints will label you as a "snob."

Many of our Asian clients have difficulties finding topics for conversation during networking events. As a result, sometimes they choose not to attend the event altogether. For them, keeping up with what is happening in sports is a way to easily start a conversation. A good way to learn about recent sports news is to watch ESPN SportsCenter [sports station on TV] which will give you the highlights of each sport, including the relays of the day's best sports' moments. You can also go to Google or ESPN.com. In addition, you can add the local teams to http://www.MyYahoo.com and check the games' outcomes there.

There are also sports bars you can go to with colleagues after work and watch TV games over a beer. Popular choices are Monday Night Football in football season, and the World Series for baseball during the playoffs for the baseball season. This is when the teams are at their best and the excitement is the highest. Don't forget to get involved in basketball as well; March Madness happens every year and has many enthusiasts.

Besides sports, other good conversation starters are general questions like, "Have you been to these events before?" "How did you hear about this event?" or "What other organizations do you belong to?"

Listen Actively

You need to learn to listen actively. This can be challenging especially for Asian women, who are used to a more passive listening style. Several of our female (and of course, some male) Asian clients would listen attentively, but show no reaction at all at the end of a segment of the conversation. No eye contact; no agreement or disagreement. If you do that, your counterpart will have no idea what you are thinking, whether you are in agreement or not, how you are feeling, etc. and will move on to someone else.

We worked with these clients on how to show greater engagement, for example by nodding their heads in conversation, saying something like "Oh, really?" or other encouraging sounds, just to show that they were participating and not just sitting there politely, but not engaged. For more on listening techniques, see Chapter 7.

Don't Interrupt

Many of us come from cultures in which it is fine to interrupt to add to a story or to pull the conversation over to ourselves. But that is not well received here. Wait for the other person to finish not only their sentence, but also their thought. If you keep interrupting other people, you will notice that very few of them will be happy to carry on a conversation with you, and that many will gingerly excuse themselves… and you will wind up standing alone.

Also, don't dominate the conversation—a frequent mistake for foreigners. Give people a chance to talk, comment, interject their remarks in between your segments of conversation.

Use Simple Language

Simple doesn't mean simplistic, just conversational.

Many international professionals have a tendency to show off their eloquence or erudition, which leaves most Americans puzzled or even annoyed. Such deliberate attempts to "star" in front of others will likely be perceived as self-aggrandizing and won't help you become well integrated in the group.

It is best to keep your message simple and adjust your vocabulary to that of the others around you. Resist the temptation to launch into heated and complex arguments, as this is not the place to talk about your political opinions. Americans in general don't appreciate over-animated discussions at networking events.

Watch yourself when you speak to make sure you are speaking clearly and slowly. Poor pronunciation will make it harder for others to understand you and, therefore, harder for you to truly connect with others.

When you are asked, "How are you?" remember that the standard answer is "Great!" Nobody expects a real answer, especially if it's not a positive one.

Be Polite

In the U.S., being polite in business (and social) conversations is very important.

Arguing is a sin here, at least arguing in a heated way, which is different from having a rational discussion.

For example, if a European starts an argument with an American and he is debating heatedly, the American will usually back off—physically removing himself or herself. The European will probably think that his/her American "friend" doesn't really care about the topic, is non-committal, perhaps superficial or even ignorant about the issue. Meanwhile, the American will think, "No way do I want to keep talking to this rude, loud person. He is putting me on the defensive. He takes himself much too seriously—I don't want to have anything to do with him."

Be Genuine

Keep in mind that networking is not selling, nor—as some Europeans suspect—is it a way to use people. You are there to try to form a relationship that lasts and is beneficial to all people involved.

It's important to act genuinely in the interest of others, not just yourself. Everyone can spot a "phony" [someone who just wants to make connections in order to advance him or herself]; so when you approach people at an event, be genuinely interested in them and in what they do, listen attentively, ask pertinent questions, and remember the answers! Faking interest won't get you very far in your attempts to make connections.

As a foreigner, don't try to impress other attendees with a list of your degrees or credentials. Many people attending professional networking events have high educational levels (which they don't usually broadcast).

Moving On

After you have spoken to someone for a while, it is fine to start looking around for other groups you can join. Don't be afraid to move on to someone new in the room. If your contact of the moment is sticking to you and you would like to move to others, you can excuse yourself and say you are going to get something to drink or eat and leave—or you can take him/her along to the new group.

Body Language

Shaking Hands

It depends on the group, as people will indeed often shake hands—but not always. You should take a cue from the other participants. If you are comfortable shaking hands (as most Europeans are, for example) do so, but not as frequently as you would do overseas.

A handshake at the first meeting is common, but further meetings are usually more casual and end with a wave, a glance and a friendly goodbye and don't need further physical contact.

Your handshake should be firm: not too hard, not too mushy. Americans, as Europeans do, place a great emphasis on a firm handshake.

Smiling

When you come to talk to one person or many, smile when you introduce yourself. If you look too serious, you won't encourage others to make contact with you.

Respecting Personal Space

In general, in the U.S. personal space is 18 inches (about 50 centimeters) between two people who are talking to each other or waiting in line; standing closer can make people feel uncomfortable. Consider at least an arm's length.

Women can usually be more physical with other women, and it's typical to exchange a kiss or a hug if they know each other well. Men usually don't have any physical contact. If they do hug, they will rapidly pat each other's back until both disengage.

Personal Appearance

Dress appropriately for an event. The main rule is to dress like the person you most respect in the company/office. If he or she wouldn't wear what you're wearing, it's probably not a good idea for you to do it.

Err on the side of conservative. For more on dress codes, see Chapter 7.

Tools of the Trade

Business Cards

Always bring your business cards with you. Even if you are unemployed and new to the U.S., bring a card with your name, your job title (or profession), the business you work for, an address, phone number, and e-mail address where people can reach you—maybe a one-liner explaining what your business is about.

Make sure your card is current and have an extra supply of cards handy. You can always print new ones inexpensively or order them on the Internet.

When you hand out your business card, always collect one in return. The exchange of business cards is a pretty low-key transaction here, not an elaborate ritual as in some other cultures, so keep it casual and brief. However, if you are exchanging a business card with someone from an Asian country, take that extra second, look at the card with attention, and put it away carefully.

Calendar

Try to go to the networking event with your working calendar, so that you can check it when you are committing to a new rendezvous. People tend to check their PDAs quickly and on the spot before scheduling a follow up meeting.

Following Up

If you promised to call, send some information, have agreed to set up breakfast or lunch, remember to do so! If you fail to follow up on your commitments, you will be ineffective in that group and no one will take your seriously.

How to Network Effectively with Colleagues or Coworkers in the Workplace

Networking with colleagues in Europe is typically a formal affair.

Take Milan or Paris: everybody is well dressed for a lunch or a dinner at a nice restaurant. People tend to stick with a group of colleagues with whom they are already familiar, engaging in spontaneous social conversation, and perhaps making plans for an outing after hours. Leisurely walking back to the office is fairly common.

Very different atmosphere in Silicon Valley (or in the U.S. in general).

Networking with colleagues will typically take place at a so-called "office lunch," either in the office lunchroom or another available conference room. The menu features pizza takeout, salad, and sodas. People put their food onto paper plates, grab a can of soda or a bottle of water, and join a group of colleagues. They might talk about sports and then seek out a colleague to get an update on how the project is going, all the while balancing their pizza, salad, and drink, and at the same checking their BlackBerry for any urgent messages. After about half an hour, they have to go to a meeting and make plans to have coffee "some time" next week.

Cultivate Your Social Skills

Many foreign professionals—for example, Asians or Hispanics—who move to the U.S. tend to hang out [spend their time] together most of the time and don't make a conscious effort to get to know their American colleagues better. The problem is that they then feel isolated and aren't sure how to make new connections. It is important for them to switch gears, to deliberately network with their (American) coworkers, and take the initiative to establish a relationship.

What can they do differently?

They could go to lunch with their team and, if possible, with their direct supervisors so he or she can get to know them as individuals, and not just as someone who works with or for them. Inviting the boss out for lunch may feel awkward to foreigners: Europeans may perceive it as an attempt to stand out; Asians may consider it inappropriate to reach beyond their hierarchical level. But it is fairly normal in the U.S. and can lead to a strong mentoring relationship.

Be Polite and Nice to Everyone

Know that assistants are the gatekeepers to their bosses, and besides being polite, it is important that you know them by name. Many people tend to ignore the receptionist, the mailroom clerk, the IT people, and others whose jobs don't seem important. Don't underestimate their power or their network of friends.

Be mindful of the language you use. Rude, rough language is never acceptable, even if other people around you use it. In most cases, female colleagues, supervisors, and bosses are very uncomfortable with inappropriate language—so just avoid it.

The office space layout may be deceivingly open and egalitarian. Still, when you approach a colleague's cubicle, always ask if that is a good time to be interrupting him or her. Keep your voice low, otherwise what you say will be heard on the entire floor. When you're in someone else's cubicle, don't hang over their shoulder and peer over at personal e-mails or documents lying on the desk.

Keep the small talk general. You're trying to get to know your colleagues, not know their DNA. It's good to remember what people tell you about their personal lives, and ask pertinent questions without being intrusive.

Therefore, no talk about politics, health, religion, salary, age, weight, sexual preferences… no questions that are too personal.

Don't Gossip

Gossiping may be a good way to stay informed informally in your native culture, especially if you come from a high-context culture (see Chapter 2). But it is not acceptable in the U.S. While it is true that it is important to be "plugged into" [be informed of] what's going on in your company through various channels of information (beyond the official ones), it is also true that gossiping will not win you any friends here. So just don't do it.

USEFUL TIPS FOR NETWORKING IN THE U.S.

Helpful
Networking regularly
Taking friends to networking events
Having a good elevator pitch
Being in a good mood, having fun
Preparing for the event (conversation topics)
Having plenty of business cards
Following up
Attending the same groups regularly
Harmful
Talking only about yourself
Trying to impress
Dominating the conversation
Monopolizing people
Not knowing how to make small talk
Sticking with one, familiar group
Not dressing appropriately
Not following up

Cultural Inventory

Check how close your values are to American ones on the following scale.

The more high scores (6) you circle, the closer your values are to American values.

If you have more low numbers, you need to be aware of the areas of difference and adjust accordingly in your business transactions.

Table 1.   CULTURAL INVENTORY*

U.S. Values	Your values					
Speak to sell/persuade	1	2	3	4	5	6
Say no clearly	1	2	3	4	5	6
Prefer explicit messages	1	2	3	4	5	6
Task oriented	1	2	3	4	5	6
Silence is difficult to handle	1	2	3	4	5	6
Rarely interrupt	1	2	3	4	5	6
Prefer direct eye contact	1	2	3	4	5	6
Short hugs, back thumpings are OK	1	2	3	4	5	6
Clear body language	1	2	3	4	5	6
Show feelings openly	1	2	3	4	5	6
Individual's work important	1	2	3	4	5	6
Self esteem is central	1	2	3	4	5	6
Focus mostly on work	1	2	3	4	5	6
Rules apply to everyone	1	2	3	4	5	6
What's right is right	1	2	3	4	5	6
Honor a contract	1	2	3	4	5	6
A deal is a deal	1	2	3	4	5	6
Prefer to use first names	1	2	3	4	5	6
We're all equal	1	2	3	4	5	6
Need space	1	2	3	4	5	6
Guard inner core from most people	1	2	3	4	5	6
Present and future are important	1	2	3	4	5	6
Time is money	1	2	3	4	5	6
Quick answers, quick solutions	1	2	3	4	5	6

Table 1.   CULTURAL INVENTORY* (continued)

U.S. Values	Your values					
Punctuality essential	1	2	3	4	5	6
One thing at a time	1	2	3	4	5	6
Many short term relationships	1	2	3	4	5	6
U.S. business culture is international	1	2	3	4	5	6
Everyone speaks business English	1	2	3	4	5	6
My way or the highway—it always works	1	2	3	4	5	6
Short term profits/fast growth emphasis	1	2	3	4	5	6
Action-oriented decision making	1	2	3	4	5	6
Negotiation based on competence	1	2	3	4	5	6
Table manners are not very important	1	2	3	4	5	6
Informality is a way of life	1	2	3	4	5	6

* Copyright © 2007 Angelika Blendstrup, Ph.D.

Bibliography

Albrecht, Maryann H., ed. International HRM: Managing Diversity in the Workplace. Malden, MA: Blackwell Publishers, 2001.

Axtell, Roger E. Dos and Taboos Around the World. 3rd edition. New York: Wiley, 1993.

Barsoux, Jean-Louis and Peter Lawrence. French Management: Elitism in Action. London, England: Cassell, 1997.

Brake, Terence, Danielle Medina Walker, and Thomas Walker. Doing Business Internationally: The Guide to Cross-Cultural Success. New York: McGraw-Hill, 1995.

Carnegie, Dale. How to Win Friends and Influence People. New York: Penguin Books, 2005.

Carté, Penny and Chris Fox. Bridging the Culture Gap. London: Kogan Page, 2004.

Engholm, Christopher and Diana Rowland. International Excellence: Seven Breakthrough Strategies for Personal and Professional Success. New York: Kodansha America Inc., 1996.

English-Lueck, J. A. A. Cultures@siliconvalley. Stanford, CA: Stanford University Press, 2002.

Elashmawi, Farid and Philip R. Harris. Multicultural Management 2000. Houston: Gold Publishing Company, 1998.

Faul, Stephanie. The Xenophobe's Guide to the Americans. Partridge Green, UK: Ravette Publishing, 1995.

Ferraro, Gary P. The Cultural Dimension of International Business, 4th edition. Upper Saddle River, NJ: Prentice Hall, 2002.

Ferrazzi, Keith. Never Eat Alone. New York: Doubleday, 2005.

Hall, Edward T. Beyond Culture. New York: Doubleday, 1981.

Hall, Edward T. and Mildred Reed Hall. Understanding Cultural Differences: Germans, French and Americans. Boston: Intercultural Press, 1999.

Harris, Philip R. and Robert T. Moran. Managing Cultural Differences: Leadership Strategies for a New World of Business. 4th edition. Houston, TX: Gulf Publishing, 1996.

Hodge, Sheida. Global Smarts: The Art of Communicating and Deal Making ANYWHERE in the World. New York: John Wiley & Sons, 2000

Hofstede, Gert Jan, Paul B. Pedersen, and Geert Hofstede. Exploring Culture. Boston: Intercultural Press, 2002.

Kets de Vries, F. R. Manfred, and Elizabeth Florent-Treacy. The New Global Leaders: Richard Branson, Percy Bernvik, and David Simon and the Remaking of International Business. San Francisco: Jossey-Bass, 1999.

Leaptrott, Nan. Rules of the Game: Global Business Protocol. Cincinnati, OH: Thomson Executive Press, 1996.

Lewis, Richard D. The Cultural Imperative: Global Trends in the 21st Century. Boston: Intercultural Press, 2003.

Lewis, Richard D. When Cultures Collide. 3rd edition, London: Nicholas Brealey Publishing, 2006.

      Bibliography

Maddox, Robert C. Cross-Cultural Problems in International Business: The Role of the Cultural Integration Function. Westport, CT: Quorum Books, 1993.

Mead, Richard. International Management: Cross-Cultural Dimensions. Cambridge, MA: Blackwell Publishers, 1994.

Morrison, Terri, and Wayne A. Conaway. Kiss, Bow and Shake Hands. Avon, MA: Adams Media, 1995.

Oddou, Gary and Mendenhall, Mark (eds.). Cases in International Organizational Behavior. Malden, MA: Blackwell Publishers,1998.

Pan, Yuling, Suzanne Wong Scollon, and Ron Scollon. Professional Communication in International Settings. Malden, MA: Blackwell Publisher, 2002.

Parker, Barbara. Globalization and Business Practice: Managing Across Boundaries. Thousand Oaks, CA: Sage Publications, 1998.

Runion, Meryl. How to Use Power Phrases to Say What You Mean, Mean What You Say, and Get What You Want. New York: McGraw-Hill, 2004.

Salmovar, Larry A. and Richard B. Porter (eds.). Intercultural Communication: A Reader. 5th edition. Belmont, CA: Wadsworth Publishing Company, 1998.

Storti, Craig. Cross-Cultural Dialogues: 74 Brief Encounters with Cultural Differences. Boston: Intercultural Press, 1994.

Storti, Craig. The Art of Crossing Cultures. Boston: Intercultural Press, 1989.

Storti, Craig. Figuring Foreigners Out. Boston: Intercultural Press, 1999.

Storti, Craig. Old World, New World, Bridging Cultural Differences: Britain, France, Germany and the U.S. Boston: Intercultural Press, 2001.

The International MBA Student's Guide to the U.S. Job Search. Wet Feet Insider Guide. San Francisco: Wet Feet Inc., 2006.

Thompson, Mary Anne. Going Global. 2003.

Trompenaars, Fons and Charles Hampden-Turner. Building Cross-Cultural Competence, How to Create Wealth from Conflicting Values. New Haven, CT: Yale University Press, 2000.

Trompenaars, Fons and Charles Hampden-Turner. Riding the Waves of Culture, Understanding Diversity in Global Business. 2nd edition. New York: McGraw-Hill,1998.

Trompenaars, Fons and Charles Hampden-Turner. 21 Leaders for the 21st Century: How Innovative Leaders Manage in the Digital Age. New York: McGraw-Hill, 2002.

Weissman, Jerry. In the Line of Fire. How to Handle Tough Questions When It Counts. Upper Saddle River, NJ: Prentice Hall, 2004.

More Resources

The authors are interested in new stories and fresh anecdotes by foreign-born professionals working in the Bay Area. If you would like to contribute your ideas, please contact the authors by visiting their websites:

http://www.verba-international.com for Ms. Ghisini
http://www.professional-business-communications.com for
Ms. Blendstrup

About the Authors

Elisabetta Ghisini

Elisabetta Ghisini is a communications consultant with over 15 years of experience in the U.S. and in Europe. She specializes in international business communications and coaches senior executives on keynote speeches, corporate presentations, and media interviews. She is an instructor at the Graduate School of Business at Stanford University, where she teaches media, interviewing, and public speaking workshops.

Previously, Elisabetta was a public relations director with Burson-Marsteller, where she orchestrated the worldwide media launch of Agilent Technologies. Prior to that, she was a communications manager with the international consulting firm McKinsey & Co., where she crafted high-impact employee communications programs for multinational clients (including HP, Bank of America, Sun Microsystems).

A native of Italy, Elisabetta holds an advanced degree in German Literature from the Universita' Statale di Milano (Dottore in Lingue e Letterature Straniere Moderne). She speaks four languages and has taught business communications skills in executive training programs around the world.

Elisabetta is Co-Executive Editor of the Happy About® International Business Communications series.

Angelika Blendstrup, Ph.D.

Angelika Blendstrup, Ph.D., is the founder and principal of Blendstrup & Associates.[22] She specializes in individualized, intercultural business communications training, accent reduction, and presentation skill coaching. She works with international as well as U.S. executives to assist them in improving their written and oral communications skills, and prepares them how to write and give effective presentations.

Angelika holds a Ph.D. in Bilingual, Bicultural Education from Stanford University. She speaks five languages and has taught U.S. business communications skills to international executives both privately as well as in companies in the Silicon Valley such as DreamWorks, Sun Microsystems, Microsoft, Oracle and Cisco.

Angelika teaches classes at Stanford University on topics such as cross cultural communication, managing virtual teams and the art of interviewing successfully.

Angelika is the Co-President of *InterFrench Silicon Valley (Silicon-French)* whose goal is to merge the best features of the French and American cultures.

She is also a Co-Executive Editor of the *Happy About International Business Communications* series. Angelika can be reached at angelika.blendstrup@gmail.com.

---

22. http://www.professional-business-communications.com

Other Happy About® Books

Purchase these books at Happy About
http://happyabout.info
or at other online and physical bookstores.

Successful immigrant entrepreneurs share their inspiring stories

If you are fascinated by the Silicon Valley dream and the stories of people who shaped it, this book is a must read.

Paperback $19.95
eBook $11.95

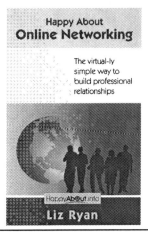

Learn the rules of successful online networking!

Whether you are a novice or expert online networker, there are tips and techniques in this book you can immediately put to use.

Paperback $19.95
eBook $11.95

Projects are MESSY!

From the minute the project begins, all manner of changes, surprises and disasters befall them. Unfortunately most of these are PREDICTABLE and AVOIDABLE.

Paperback $19.95
eBook $11.95

Learn the 42 Rules of Marketing!

Compilation of ideas, theories and practical approaches to marketing challenges that marketers know they should do, but don't always have the time or patience for.

Paperback $19.95
eBook $11.95

Printed in the United States
200820BV00002B/181-252/A

9 781600 050732